Church-Folk
Some
Messed-Up-Folk

To Jim

It's been a pleasure working with you these last three decades.

May God ever Bless you

Dr. Louis Timms

(TL)

Church-Folk
Some
Messed-Up-Folk

◆

One Man's Journey from Faith to Faith

Nevertheless the Foundation of God Standeth Sure
2 Timothy 2:19

Dr. Louis Timm's

iUniverse, Inc.
New York Lincoln Shanghai

Church-Folk Some Messed-Up-Folk
One Man's Journey from Faith to Faith

iUniverse, Inc.

For information address:
iUniverse, Inc.
2021 Pine Lake Road, Suite 100
Lincoln, NE 68512
www.iuniverse.com

ISBN: 0-595-33230-7 (pbk)
ISBN: 0-595-66785-6 (cloth)

Printed in the United States of America

Dedicated

To my Beloved Bishop

"THE HONORABLE BISHOP E.D.M."

We are not perfect, we are just forgiven.

Contents

INTRODUCTION ix

CHAPTER 1   "KNOWING THE MAIN CHARACTER" 1

CHAPTER 2   "SOME BACKGROUND HISTORY" 20

CHAPTER 3   "SOME FINANCIAL INFORMATION" 42

CHAPTER 4   "THE SUN IS GOING DOWN" 58

CHAPTER 5   "THE END OF AN ERA" 69

CHAPTER 6   "A TALE OF TWO DEATHS" 79

CHAPTER 7   "A THREEFOLD CORD IS BROKEN" 96

CHAPTER 8   "THE CALM BEFORE THE STORM" 106

CHAPTER 9   "THE EYE OF THE STORM" 121

CHAPTER 10   "THE STORM IS PASSING OVER" 144

CHAPTER 11   "DIVINE REVELATIONS" 152

CHAPTER 12   "DIVINE DELIVERANCE" 167

CHAPTER 13   "DIVINE JUDGMENT" 175

CHAPTER 14   "PROPER PERSPECTIVES" 183

CHAPTER 15   "IT IS WELL, WITH MY SOUL" 195

CONCLUSION 207

INTRODUCTION

Louis had first began writing a book in 1994, but not wanting to throw off on anyone, he threw the entire manuscript away, not even keeping a rough draft for himself. For the past ten years, he had given little or no thought at all to writing a book. As time had passed on however, and so much had now happened in his life, his spirit was again awakened within, and a renewed sense of wanting to write a book took a hold of him once again, so on Saturday, May 15[th,] 2004, while driving home from the weekly dinner that he usually had with his parents, his spirit became really restless. This particular Saturday, his mother was in Georgia for the wedding of one of her five sisters, so he had gone over to have dinner with his father.

While driving home that evening, it weighed so heavily in his spirit, that again, he was to began writing a book, it was almost as if he heard an audible voice. Since so much time had now passed, some of the anger that he had previously held onto had also subsided. At this time, the title also weighed very heavily upon him in his spirit, along with a few other instructions that I'll not share at this time.

Always wanting to be obedient to the spirit of the living God, he took all these things and pondered them in his heart for about 12 hours, before even mentioning anything about this to his wife, and within 24 hours he had began writing the book.

1

"KNOWING THE MAIN CHARACTER"

1ST THESSALONIANS 5:12-13

"And we beseech you, brethren, to know them which labour among you, and are over you in the Lord, and admonish you; and to esteem them very highly in love for their work's sake. And be at peace among yourselves."

Louis woke up on Sunday May 16th, 2004 and told his wife, that while he was driving home from visiting with his father the previous evening, that the Lord had dealt with him in the spirit, and had impressed upon him in spirit, so strongly, that he was to write a book, and that the title of it was to be:

"CHURCH-FOLK SOME MESSED-UP FOLK"

As the evening progressed that Saturday, he was also given specific instructions on what to write, and how long the book was to be. He was told to write three pages a day, for one hundred days, and just as the Lord had given the children of Israel manna from heaven **(from the 16th chapter of Exodus)**, as a daily provision, he would also tell him what he should write.

Being the Director of Christian Education, at his church, the job of teaching the adult Sunday school class was his responsibility.

As he taught Sunday school that morning, his mind was racing 100 miles an hour, just thinking, that if he could write six pages a day, he could cut that time in half and have this done in 50 days, again the Lord spoke to him in his spirit and said, Louis, you are to write three pages a day, for one hundred days, and that just as the Lord had given the children of Israel manna from heaven, as their daily provision, he would also tell Louis exactly what he was to write, and that if for some reason on Sunday's, he did not have the time to write, then the day before, or the following day, the Lord would give him two days worth of material to write.

Louis and his sister Delilah (who also teaches Sunday school), had also just been discussing discipline among ministers, concerning being led by the spirit of God, following and adhering to his word, which I will elaborate on this later in the book and tie it in with this.

See what I mean, why couldn't he just do what the Lord had told him to do?

Because "He's church-folk", and

"CHURCH-FOLK SOME MESSED-UP FOLK"

So much had gone on in Louis's life, that the difficult task I face is deciding at which point to arbitrarily start, concerning his life's journey as it pertains to dealing with church-folk. I have arbitrarily chosen the age of twenty-five, and will allude to events earlier or later as circumstances in his life dictate.

At twenty-five years of age, It was at a time in Louis's life, of mediocrity, he had a beautiful wife, two fine boys, three and five years of age, a good job, nice house and car, a right relationship with God, and a decent church life as far as he knew, however, his life was not complete, you know, when everyone else looks at you and thinks that you've got it going on, but you know that something is missing. What I have learned, and many of you already know this, is that anytime you have a gut feeling that something is wrong, it probably is.

Louis was awakened by the smell of breakfast, this particular summer Sunday morning, in 1985, nothing really out of the ordinary. He had been working six days a week and couldn't even sleep late on Sundays. You see, Louis also had the tedious task of being the Bishop of the churches assistant, and chauffer. He also knew that for the Bishop, no excuse would suffice if you were not at his door by 9:00 A.M., to pick him up for Sunday School and morning worship services. I should know, how?, because,

"I'M THE BELOVED BISHOP"

I had come to pastor the church there, when Louis was only four years old, and early on, God had shown me, that there was a difference in this young man, pretty much like God himself had commended Caleb in the bible,

Numbers 14:24

"But my servant Caleb, because he had another spirit with him, and hath followed me fully, him will I bring into the land whereinto he went; and his seed shall possess it."

I saw another spirit in Louis, therefore I kept him always before the Lord in prayer, you would be surprised, at what the Lord can do in the life of one individual, whose life is yielded completely to him, who earnestly seeks God, and to know and to do his perfect will.

I remember when Louis was eleven years old, my secretary showed me one of his tithe envelopes, it had a quarter in it, we laughed, he couldn't even spell tithes, he spelled it tides, but I saw in him a young man with a pure heart.

This particular Saturday, Louis and Carol, that's his wife, had attended a wedding and reception for friends that Carol had grown up with, they were out late, then had to pick the boys up from their maternal grandparents house, and by the time they had gotten home and to bed, it was after 1:00 A.M., Louis was not a happy camper, but when all was said and done, the four of them were up and dressed, and were there to pick me up by their normal 9:00 A.M.

Church was fine, Louis is now approaching the end of his second year as the Sunday School secretary, as usual I preached hard that sermon, this is what the people have become accustomed to, and seeing as though in a few months I'll be eighty years old, its beginning to take its toll on me, the subject that day was;

"Sin in the camp" (from the 7th chapter of Joshua).

God had really preserved me, and I knew that Louis had admired and looked up to me every since I had first come there when he was only four years old, as an adult he had always known that I loved him, but at times I could be very critical, not just of him, but of everyone, why?, because in my life people have not always been kind to me, there is, and always will be, those that sit around and judge you and your motives, always trying to find fault in you and your testimony, however, Louis had always treated me with the utmost respect, therefore, he had always known that I had prayed for him on a constant basis, he also knew that I had told his parents that I had adopted him, and that he was now my son, as well as theirs. Most Sundays are extremely long though, for both of us, luckily he and I live on the same side of town.

Louis normally leaves home around 8:45 A.M., picks me up at 9:00 A.M., we usually arrive at the church for Sunday School which starts at 9:30 A.M., it ends, and church begins around 11:00 A.M., it ends around 2:00 P.M., he usually runs out to get something to eat, comes back for evening service from approximately 4:00 P.M. to 6:00 P.M., we break from about 6:00 P.M. to 7:00 P.M., and night service usually lasts from 7:00 P.M. to about 9:30 P.M., and I want someone there with me at all times, and its usually Louis.

After night service, everybody wants to shake my hand and tell me their whole life story, that thirteen of their sixteen sons are in jail, four of their eight daughters are pregnant with their second or third child, but praise God, one of them is now contemplating marriage, their husbands are acting up, and everybody needs a special prayer, with the laying on of hands.

Well it is now almost 10:00 P.M., we finally leave the church headed for home, Louis drops me off somewhere around 10:30 P.M., and he and his family arrive back at their home about 10:45 P.M. Well guess what, he gets to get up in the morning, work six days this week, and do it all over again the next week, and as most of you church-folk should know, Louis knows all of your business, how?, because I'm the Bishop, and I tell him that's how, why?, because, I'm church-folk also, and:

"CHURCH-FOLK SOME MESSED-UP FOLK"

Louis's wife Carol, had been extremely nice to him all that week, she had submitted herself to him every single night that week, talk about the twilight zone, he thought to himself, she must really be starting to like me. Marriage is a real job, its been said, that you must work at it like a business, and the only place that a business will run itself, is downhill, it has also been said, that marriage is like flies on a screen door, those inside want out, and those outside want to get in.

Their first few years had been pretty rocky, you know there's that adjustment period, where the two of you are getting to know one another, and what each others limitations are, what each will, and will not accept, things seemed to be going pretty smooth for them now, I just pray, that its not the calm before the storm.

Louis had really always wanted a stay at home wife, but do to circumstances, that wasn't really possible at this time.

But God has been very good to the both of them, and they were blessed that she only had to work twenty hours a week. For the first few years she did not work at all, but finances got pretty tight, and she was forced out into the workplace.

When the recession came in the early 1980's, work had slowed down for Louis, and for two years, he was only working four days a week, he began to use his credit cards just to keep things going, And just when he was at the end of his finances, when the credit cards were all maxed out, and when bankruptcy was looking pretty darn attractive, all of a sudden, the economy picked up, and he went from working four days a week, to six days a week, almost immediately.

He was in such heavy debt now, that it seemed he'd still be paying off the credit cards when Jesus comes back.

As a man, it seems that when we can't provide for our family, and to even be there at times for our extended families, we tend to have feelings of insecurity and inferiority. Many a man has gotten himself into more debt than he can get himself out of, simply because we don't want our family or friends, to think that we of all people, are having financial difficulties, and God forbid that the wife should find out, some women can cut you to the quick, and can make you feel worst than a little child, especially after she has already told Sister Lady at church, that she was pledging $1,000 for the building fund, trust me that money is coming from somewhere, and she doesn't really care where it comes from.

When we began to spend and spend, we develop habits, so that when the money gets tight, or takes evasive maneuvers altogether, our habits may not change in a timely enough fashion to help us avoid a head on collision with certain disaster, we hide the fact that we're in trouble.

We tend to believe that a knight in shining armor, is coming to the rescue, that the lottery God is going to smile down on us, and by the time most of us are willing to admit it, we're in so deep, that we couldn't hide it anymore if we wanted to. Been there, done that.

We must learn a valuable lesson from these trying times that will come into all of our lives, they will not only make us a better people, they will also make us better able to cope with the many other disappointments that will come, the next time they come into our lives. If you haven't experienced hard times, keep living, if and when possible, learn from the mistakes of others, you can't possibly live long enough to make them all yourself.

Louis and Carol's oldest son Junior, starts school this year, their other son Byron, has the task of being the ring bearer in a family friends wedding that summer. The bride to be, just happens to be Junior's God-sister, Tina. So why did she choose Byron instead of Junior, she said that she thought he was smaller, and that he would look so much cuter if we could persuade him to do it, if not, Junior was her second choice. Tina has always been kind of a loner, and doesn't have a lot of friends, neither does Rick, the guy she's marrying, so she has asked many of the young men at church if they would stand in and be his groomsmen, when it came down to needing one more man, Louis told Tina that he was very surprised to find that they had asked a new member, instead of asking him, I'll tell you her response later, I promise.

Tina's mother, Ms Booker, and Louis, have always been very fond of each other, that's why when Junior was born, he told her, that he wanted her to be Junior's God-mother. The wedding was absolutely beautiful, a wedding that Tina later confided in Louis, should never have happened at all, she said that the week before the wedding she knew that she was making a terrible mistake, and wanted to call it off, but do to pressure from church-folk, telling her that she just had cold feet, she went on ahead and married him anyway. It turned out that her fears were well founded, that marriage lasted about a year. You know what,

"CHURCH-FOLK SOME MESSED-UP FOLK"

Later that year, Louis also allowed two of his sisters to talk him into something that he doesn't normally do, that is, to miss a day from work, he'd only ever missed one day in six years, and that was during his second year when he'd had three wisdom teeth extracted.

There was a vacation resort about 100 miles away, that they were all going to visit that Friday, and people know how to mess with you psychologically, you know the mind games they play, telling you that you deserve a day off, you deserve to treat yourself, just call in and tell them you're sick, they'll understand.

Naive Louis, he did it, and on many jobs like this, that don't have a union, where certain things can be gotten away with, you know where the rules can be bent, but there's always a price to pay, remember, that for every action, there is an opposite and equal reaction. For those of you that understand piecework jobs, certain machines may be a little easier to run, or the pieces produced may pay you a little more per piece to run them, this is the kind of job that Louis had.

Louis returned to work that Monday, and was told that the Friday he had called in sick, someone else had to run the machine that he normally ran, and that now, that individual had been given the machine permanently, he now would be moved to this individuals old machine. That one Friday off, resulted in a five thousand dollar a year pay cut for Louis.

To thine own self be true, Louis couldn't blame anyone but himself, just as with any sin, God has given each and everyone of us the freedom of choice, and the power to say yes or no, lies within each and everyone of us, just as the choice is ours, we must remember, so is the consequence. I don't care what anyone tells you, there is a consequence for sin. So when you see certain individuals, living in open, or secret sin for that matter, and all seems to be going well with them, think about what the word of God says,

Isaiah 55:11

"So shall my word be that goeth forth out of my mouth: it shall not return unto me void, but it shall accomplish that which I please, and it shall prosper in the thing whereto I sent it."

Numbers 32:23

"But if ye will not do so, behold, ye have sinned against the Lord; and be sure your sin will find you out."

You have no idea of the inner struggle and turmoil, that some individuals are going through at any given time, but God knows, his vision is better than ours, and he doesn't look on the outside as man does, he sees beyond the facades that we may be able to put up to fool people, he sees past that it is well with my soul look, he sees past that stoic look that tells people, I've got it all together, we can't fool him, remember in his foolishness, he still outshines us in our wisdom:

1st Corinthians 1:25

"Because the foolishness of God is wiser than men; and the weakness of God is stronger than men."

Oh bless his name.

The latter part of that same year, Louis had a neighbor named Mr. Smith, whom had lived there since 1961, he had a burglary at his home, and he came over and knocked on Louis's door about 7:00 A.M., this was around the first week of November, and he began to tell Louis that about 3:00 A.M. that morning, three black men wearing ski masks, had broken into his home, he said that they had broken the front window, and came in through the living room, and that as he was lying in bed, he heard the glass break, he jumped up, reached over and grabbed his pants, bent down to put them on, and rose, to see a gun pointed directly at his head.

One of the men yelled a profanity at another, and they told Mr. Smith to give them his wallet, he complied, and they left. Louis asked him, if they were wearing ski masks how could he possibly know that they were black, by their hands he told him, they didn't have anything on them. Mr. Smith was sixty-six years old, and very grateful to just escape with his life. The only reason he had come over to bother Louis at all, was the fact that before they had broken in, they had cut his telephone lines, and he needed to use Louis's telephone to now call the authorities. Louis asked him, if they broke in around 3:00 A.M., and its now 7:00 A.M, why didn't he come over sooner, Mr. Smith told him that he did not want to disturb him, and that he had been trying to wait until saw a light come on, or some signs of life, so that he would know that they were awake.

Within the hour, four cars from the detective unit were there, and they spent a good portion of their day over there. Louis had just told his wife Carol earlier that same week, that she had to quit being so careless, and then that very morning, as he went to turn the alarm off, it was already off, upon questioning Carol, she said that she had gotten up to use the bathroom, turned it off, and forgot to turn it back on.

Mr. Smith called Louis over, later that evening to tell him, that he would never be spending another night in that house, and that he had a lady friend, whom Louis had often seen over there, she had a two bedroom apartment not to far from there, and that he would be moving in with her, and that since her apartment was equipped with everything they needed, most of the furnishings in his home were no longer needed, he gave Louis his washer, dryer, stove, refrigerator, humidifier, Kirby vacuum cleaner, numerous dishes and knickknacks, and the coffee pot, which after nearly twenty years, Louis still uses to this day.

God has always opened the windows of heaven to Louis, and my constant and continual prayer to God is, that his presence will ever be with him. Louis asked Mr. Smith what his plans were for the house, if he wasn't going to be living there anymore, he gave Louis a business card, from a real estate company, which he had called a few hours earlier, and said that they had already came out and purchased the house from him, cash on the spot, they gave him forty-five percent of what the home was worth.

Mr. Smith had a large motor-home, and he had built a large oversized garage to keep it in, that garage alone cost him almost as much as he sold the entire house for, he told Louis that all he was trying to get, was what he and his mother had paid for the house when they purchased it in 1961. He sold it to the real estate company, and six weeks later, they sold it to a young couple with two children, the husbands fourteen year old brother also lived with them. So what does this have to do with church-folk, you'll understand it better as the story unfolds.

Whether you belong to a large congregation or a small congregation, you'll have your share of garbage and messy folks in the church, I've found that the only difference is that with a large congregation, you've usually got a big mess on your hands, and usually with a small congregation, you've got a little mess on your hands, note the operative word here is usually. As long as we are in the flesh, there's going to be messy folk, in and out of the church, however in all that we say and do, let us try to be a part of the solution, and not of the problem, it has been said that life is ten percent action, and ninety percent reaction, be careful how you react to messy-folk, don't give them what they want, don't keep the fire burning for them.

What Louis has learned in his journey through life, is that many people, have told him many things, hoping that he would keep it going, with some things, no, in all things, we must ask the Lord to give us a discerning spirit, we must remember, that the honest, sincere, God loving, genuine, church going Christians, are still human.

Many times we may look at our loved ones, or co-workers, or ex-church members, and wonder why they have seemingly given up on God and on the church, come on people, lets look at the kind of representatives we've been to, and for God, if your father owned a company, and it was your job to represent the company, and build it up, knowing that one day this would be yours for an inheritance, would you really want you for a representative, if most of us represented a company, the way that we have represented God, the company would soon go bankrupt, that, in and of itself alone, should say something to us about our representation of, and dedication to God.

Leviticus 10:10

"And that ye may put difference between holy and unholy, and between unclean and clean"

There are many people, that we come into contact with on a daily basis, who would be shocked to find out, that some of us were card carrying, born-again, usher board serving, Sunday-school teaching, holy rolling and shouting, tongue-talking saints. I'm not saying that you should wear a three-inch cross, or write the word Christian on your forehead, I'm simply saying, that if you're saved, you ought to show some signs, there should be something different, that people will see in you, that they just don't see in the rest of the world.

The more people I meet and talk to, the more I like my dog, the more I also see, that everyone has his or her own story, with a different set of tailor-made problems, made just for them, what I've found is, that when an individual is going through something, to that individual, and at that particular time, to them it is very traumatic, but we in our finiteness, want to minimize everyone else's problem, while maximizing our own, we have learned to give advice by the bucket, while at the same time, taking it by the grain, we have become such a self-centered, self-serving society, that we as individuals, I believe, are really beginning to feel that the world revolves around each and every one of our lives, we have become to God, what we ourselves are raising in our own children, a generation with an entitlement mentality.

Jesus Christ, in his sermon on the mount taught the beatitudes (**from the 5th chapter of Matthew**), some of us have now changed this to the me-attitudes, we live as if we think the world owes us something, the least little bit of discomfort or pain that we face, we believe that the world has somehow wronged us. Think about it, what have we really done, to make us believe that everything should always go our way, are we really that pleased with ourselves, or is it possible, that we are just that disillusioned with life.

Louis was brought up in the church, therefore most of his social life involves church, church-folk, or family.

Its two weeks before thanksgiving and Jim and Lydia, a young couple at the church are getting married, Lydia and Louis have known each other their entire lives, at one time they sort of had a thing for each other, when they were teenagers, both their entire families are very close, almost like kinfolk, she's the lead singer in the church choir, and that girl knows that she can sang, Jim, well honestly no one seems to know where he came from, no one seems to know anything about him, no one seems to know anything about his background, I put him right up there with Melchizedek:

Hebrews 7:3

"Without father, without mother, without descent, having neither beginning of days, nor end of life."

Some people have said that they think that he is strange, if you know what I mean, I do know this about him, that he is one of the most talented, if not the most talented, musicians that I have ever heard before. They have made our choir, one of the greatest, in this city.

I do not know, for the life of me exactly what went on with the two of them, but there was a young man named Paul, who sometimes came to visit the church, he and Lydia knew each other rather well, he also was a very talented musician, and he would occasionally stop by and play the organ for the choir, even when he didn't stay for the church services. This was all before Lydia met Jim, and became engaged to him.

Well who would have thought it, Paul showed up at the wedding, someone told me that he had had a few drinks in him, and he told everyone at the church, that he knew Jim, and that he had come to talk to Lydia, to put a stop to this wedding, talk about quiet, the whole church was so quiet that you could literally hear someone's heart beating. Somebody went and told Jim about it, and he came upstairs and literally threw Paul out of the church, he said that there is no Devil in hell that's going to stop this wedding.

One year, I didn't have anyone to drive me to our big annual church meeting in the south, Jim volunteered and said that he would drive me, and that he did. I told Louis that he could be sure that this would never happen again, every time I looked for Jim, he'd be gone somewhere in my car, with some of the strange men, if you know what I mean, from the church hosting the annual meeting. This meeting normally ran ten days straight, and services were usually held from 10:00 A.M. to 11:00 P.M. daily, with short intermissions, much like our Sunday services, one of the things that upsets me is, I buy Louis a brand new Cadillac every three years, and wherever I am, I like the car to be there also, that way, everyone knows that when they see the car, that I am also there, that even applies to Louis on Sundays, I want him and the car there with me, the whole day.

By the way, Paul was a little strange also, and two years after Lydia and Jim were married, he died of AIDS.

Back to Jim and Lydia, after the wedding, they were at the table talking to Louis's sister Delilah, Louis walked over just as Delilah was asking them, what were their honeymoon plans that evening, well Jim said, we had talked about getting a room downtown for the night, but spending on the wedding had gotten a little out of hand, and money was now a little too tight for comfort, so we really don't know what we're going to do tonight. Wouldn't you know it, Delilah had the most brilliant idea, why don't the two of you go over and stay at Louis and Carol's house tonight, and the four of them can just come over and spend the night at my house, Louis could have messed in his pants, because now, everyone's looking at him, Louis said that they wouldn't want to stay at his house, yes we would said Jim, well Louis said, this is such short notice, just let me think about it.

Delilah told Louis, that all he needed to do, was just go home and get them something to sleep in, and come on over, but its Saturday night Louis said, and all of you know that Sunday mornings are very busy at my house, plus I have to pick Bishop up by 9:00 A.M. he said, I'll wake you up in plenty of time said Delilah, and we'll be up and ready to leave by the time you get home said Jim, now how am I going to get out of this one, Louis thought, he saw his last hope standing across the room, well let me check with Carol and I'll let you know he said, Carol, Lydia hollered across the room, could you come over here please, go ahead and ask her Louis, said Lydia, look, I have a better idea Louis said, why don't I give you the money to get a room for the night, no said Lydia, ask Carol, well Carol, Louis said, Delilah had this brilliant idea, that Jim and Lydia could use our house for their honeymoon tonight, she also said that you and I, along with the boys could come over and spend the night at her house, Ohh, Carol exclaimed, what an excellent idea, Lydia, you can follow us home after the reception, we'll grab a few things, and be out of the house in no time, Louis thought to himself, Carol and Delilah both must have mental problems. When he told me about it, I told him that he must have one too.

I've told Louis, time and time again, don't let anyone pressure you into doing anything that you do not want to do. So after the reception, off they went home, Louis, Carol and the boys, got their pajamas, a couple of other things, and headed over to Delilah's, where the four of them slept on the cold, hard, living room floor. Louis tossed and turned the entire night, just thinking about the fact, that he and his family, had nice warm beds at home, with someone else in them.

Louis had told Delilah that night, that if she never spoke to him again, that would probably be too soon, she thought that all of this was extremely amusing, you know what she had the nerve to tell him, you wouldn't believe it, listen to this revelation, Delilah said, Louis, all you had to do, was to just say no.

Why couldn't He just say no, this is something that we as Christians must learn, that we all have choices, and that at times, there is nothing wrong with simply saying no, we continue to let people ramrod us into serving on committees, and volunteering us for the things that they themselves don't want to do.

That next morning Louis was up and out of Delilah's house before 7:00 A.M., needless to say, Jim and Lydia were not up and dressed as they had promised they would be, Louis, Carol, and the children, had to get ready around them, and they did make it to my house on time that morning. At church Louis told Delilah that she had better not even look at him. Why? Because,

"CHURCH-FOLK SOME MESSED-UP FOLK"

Where did the time go, its almost Christmas, and Louis hasn't done a thing to prepare for it This is the one time of year, every year, that I think he wishes, he were a Jehovah's Witness, as are most of his relatives, on his mother and fathers sides. He said that too often, people go out and buy too many things that they don't really need, with money that they don' really have.

Louis has been trying to help out his brother Michael's wife Janet, and their children, Michael had gotten himself into some trouble, and was sent off to prison last year, so they would all try, very successfully I might add, to put Louis on a guilt trip, and try to make him think that they were now his responsibility.

There is nothing at all wrong with helping others out, the problem is, knowing where to draw the line, as you'll see later, Louis has had a problem with drawing that line for a very long time. Church-folk will take the shirt off your back, if you let them, when is enough, really enough.

This year, Louis said that he was going to take his entire family out to dinner, nieces, nephews and all, because he really felt with all of his heart, that when God blesses you, out of mere gratitude, you should want to share it with someone else. He took the entire family to the Brown Derby restaurant, and maybe this is just me, but personally, I have always felt, that anything I wouldn't do with my own money, I certainly wouldn't do it with someone else's, unfortunately, everyone does not share that feeling, Louis sat back in awe, and watched, as they ordered their food, and told their children to order anything on the menu that they wanted to, because they didn't have to pay for it, which is fine, but when was the last time that you let your seven and nine year olds order Surf & Turf, we ought not sometimes wonder why people only invite us out, or over, only once in our life.

We must, in any and all circumstances, do unto others as we would have them do unto us, needless to say, the dinner tab was quite large, and that this, was the first, and the last time that Louis ever did that for his family, at least on that widespread of a basis. You know some things in life just make you go ummm.

Their whole family grew up very, very poor, but it was their mother who had always known the true value of a dollar, when you're making twenty-four dollars a week, yes I said week, you have to learn to stretch your dollars, she worked three days a week, and earned eight dollars a day when they were children, and this mind you, provided for a family of ten, well what about their father you wander, what about their father? That should be a whole chapter all by itself.

Why is it, that when you go into a church, ninety to ninety-five percent of most of our congregations are made up of women, not all of them are single women either, but you rarely see the husbands, if you see them at all. Why, because we men are too busy trying to prove something, either to ourselves or somebody else, that we are self-sufficient, macho, egotistical, chauvinistic, needing nobody fools.

In my journey through life, what I have learned is that if you would seek God with your whole heart, and serve him to the best of your ability, that he will take you to higher heights, and deeper depths in him, according to the level of sincerity in any given individual, we know him as we follow him. If most of our wives, were as faithful to us, as we are to God, we simply would not tolerate it, think about it, most animals are more faithful to their masters, than we are to God.

We should be most careful, not to fall from grace, with God, he is slow to anger, and longsuffering according to;

2 Peter 3:9

"The Lord is not slack concerning his promise, as some men count slackness; but is longsuffering to us-ward, not willing that any should perish, but that all should come to repentance."

Please don't count it as slackness, when the Lord does not swiftly punish us in our wrongdoings, out of the abundance of his grace, that only the infinite God of the universe possesses, he is not willing that any should perish, but he is giving men everywhere the opportunity to repent. One day, every knee will bow, and every tongue will confess that Jesus Christ is Lord, to the glory of God the father, we can do it by choice, or we can do it by force, the choice is ours, for now.

Philippians 2:10-11

"That at the name of Jesus every knee should bow, of things in heaven, and things in earth, and things under the earth; and that every tongue should confess that Jesus Christ is Lord, to the glory of God the Father."

As a child, eleven years old, Louis had a bible, with a blue jean cover, his mother would often see him reading it. His hearts desire, was that the

Lord would save him from the wrath to come, he had always wanted to have a right relationship with God, but as a young man, he thought much about all the things in life that he might miss out on, he told me that he often prayed that the Lord would delay his coming long enough for him to grow up, let the Devil have his way with him, and then he would turn his life over to God.

Romans 7:24

"O wretched man that I am! Who shall deliver me from the body of this death?"

We are wretched, and how can anyone be so selfish, so self-centered, to think that the Lord of the universe, would delay his coming, for our foolishness, just let the other five billion people be put on hold for Louis sake, sounds foolish, this is the kind of mentality, that has taken hold of the masses today, what have we done that was so marvelous, so magnificent, so good or so righteous, that God should stand up and take notice, nothing, not one thing, whatever fate should deal us, should we not graciously accept it, according to:

1st John 4:19

"We love him, because he first loved us."

He left his throne in glory, took upon himself, the form of sinful man, died for my sins and yours, shed his innocent blood, that we might be atoned, rose walking in the newness of life as an example to us, that if we die, no when we die, that we shall live again, he ascended into the heavens, and is right now seated, at the right hand of God, ever making intercession for us, our past present and future sins, he is building for us a mansion, eagerly waiting for us to just accept him as our Lord and Savior, and we still have the nerve to think that we're entitled to something else, what more can he do, than that which he has already done, he has already laid the foundation, and opened up the way, if there is any failure, believe me, its not in God, its in us, its all about the choices we make, and have made, we will spend eternity somewhere.

Psalm 121:1-8

"I will lift up mine eyes unto the hills, from whence cometh my help. My help cometh from the Lord, which made heaven and earth. He will not suffer thy foot to be moved: he that keepeth thee will not slumber. Behold, he that keepeth Israel shall neither slumber nor sleep. The Lord is thy keeper: the Lord is thy shade upon thy right hand. The sun shall not smite thee by day, nor the moon by night. The Lord shall preserve thee from all evil: he shall preserve thy soul. The Lord shall preserve thy going out and thy coming in from this time forth, and even for evermore."

I prayed that throughout Louis's life, he would always make wise choices, and that the Lord, would not allow him to go out into the world and get all messed up, and entangled in a life of sin. God had been my keeper, and I knew that he could keep Louis also.

2

"SOME BACKGROUND HISTORY"

Acts 22:3

"I am verily a man which am a Jew, born in Tarsus, a city in Cilicia, yet brought up in this city at the feet of Gamaliel, and taught according to the perfect manner of the law of the fathers, and was zealous toward God, as ye all are this day."

Philippians 3:4-7

"Though I might also have confidence in the flesh. If any other man thinketh that he hath whereof he might trust in the flesh, I more. Circumcised the eighth day, of the tribe of Benjamin, an Hebrew of Hebrews; as touching the law, a Pharisee. Concerning zeal, persecuting the church; touching the righteousness which is in the law blameless. But what things were gain to me, those I counted loss for Christ."

I need you to really grasp this one point, that if you don't know where you've been, you can't possibly know where you are going, knowing an individual can help give you some insight as to the make-up of his character, and an individuals character will play a big factor in the outcome of that individuals life.

Janet is Louis's brother Michael's wife, she called to ask a favor of Louis one day, she said that someone she knew was selling a car, and that the Lord had told her to call him, and ask him, if he would buy it for her as an early Christmas present that year, first of all, how did she even know if she was getting a Christmas present that year, the bible also talks about the sin of presumption.

Now before I go any further I'd just like to know one thing, how come when God speaks to someone, they are always on the receiving end, if God really wanted someone to do something for you, why didn't he just tell that individual and cut out the middle man, I didn't think he still needed that kind of mediator, if I gave everybody, everything that they told me, that God had told them to tell me to give to them, I'd have to go out and lie to someone, and tell them, that God told me to tell them to give me something, now think about this.

How many times has someone came to you and told you that the Devil told them, to tell you, to give them something, sadly enough, more often times than not, that would probably be closer to the truth, than lying saying that God had told them, we had better try and quit blaming God for all of our mess, too many of us are serving the "Gimme God", personally, God has never told me to tell anyone else to give me anything, when God talks to or deals with me about giving, it is always about me giving something to someone else, and ninety-nine percent of the time, it catches them totally off guard.

Well anyway, now that I've got that off my chest, Janet told Louis how much money she needed for the car, and she asked him if he would be willing to give it to her, he told her to let him think about it and that he would call her later in the week to let her know, well she said, I've already told the man that I would come by and pick it up tomorrow, Louis thought to himself, I am one heck of a sucker, he told her that he would go to the bank and get it to her by tomorrow.

That's another thing, why is it that when someone wants your money, you've always got to take it to them, and if you get it back, you've got to go back and get it also, what I've learned is that most people will do to you whatever you allow them to, Louis's cousin once told him, that another cousin had called him, wanting to borrow a large amount of money, after much thought, the one cousin said that he told the other cousin, now if I loan you this money, and you don't pay it back to me, I'm going to be very upset with you, on the other hand, if I don't loan it to you, you're going to be very upset with me, well he said, I'd rather you be upset with me. That made sense to Louis, so why couldn't he take that rule and apply it to himself.

Louis did take the money over to Janet the next day, and that evening she called him, and told him that she had gone and picked the car up. He had a very good heart, but man in his fallen state, can harden very quickly.

Would you like to know what gratitude is, so would I, most people have no idea what it is, Janet drove the car to church that following Sunday, and told me, the Bishop, to make sure and come out after church, to see the piece of garbage car that Louis had bought her, and that's no lie, why, because she's church-folk, and

"CHURCH-FOLK SOME MESSED-UP FOLK"

No one can imagine how that made Louis feel, he just pondered these things in his heart. Too many of us short change ourselves, and then want to blame someone else for the things or the character that we seem to lack, no one owes us anything, not even God, and many a folk have missed out on a greater blessing because they lacked showing the gratitude that they should have in the small things, remember, a small hole can sink a great ship, and the bible says in,

Zechariah 4:10

"For who hath despised the day of small things?

Louis had another brother named Rod. Now Rod it seems, had been messed up for the most part, his whole life, I mean he's intelligent, looks a lot like Louis, but he's just always looked for the easy way out, he's never had a problem getting women, and has even managed to talk two of them into marrying him, and he's still with the second one now. Now when I say messed up, what I mean is, he's just never quite been able to get it together, I mean this thing called life, he's never really had time for God, never really had a job, I mean he's so against working, that if a job crawled into bed with him, he'd crawl out.

Occasionally Rod and Louis would have some pretty deep and in depth discussions, now keep in mind, that they are all the children of the same mother and father, before you start to wonder, but that boy Rod just isn't all there. Their mother said that as a child, she knew that Rod would be a problem, you see at five years of age, she said he was already cutting school, she did manage however, to get him to go though, for the most part until he was about twelve years old.

So what does Rod have to do with church-folk, well all of their lives, they were all brought up in the same church, their mother, has always set an exemplary example, of what the Christian life should be, but Rod was always in and out of trouble, and in and out of jail, from about the age of fourteen years old. He never really wanted to work, but he'd do just about anything else for money, and after spending so much time in and out of jail, he had become very knowledgeable about the bible, and about the precepts of God. It was in one of these deep conversations that Louis had with Rod, that Rod told him, that after reading the bible, particularly:

Revelation 7:4

"And I heard the number of them which were sealed: and there were sealed an hundred and forty and four thousand of all the tribes of the children of Israel."

Rod said that he was thoroughly convinced, that God wanted him to be a preacher during the great tribulation period, and that he would be one of those 144,000, that God would seal, and use in a special way, therefore he could live a very riotous lifestyle, and pretty much do any and everything, because it didn't really matter how he lived now, Jesus had already paid it all, and he was making sure that the Lords death would not be in vain, his sins had already been paid for, past, present and future, and he'd rectify all of this during the great tribulation period.

God does not make mistakes, if he brings you to it, he'll bring you through it, and when you accuse God of something, think long and hard about it, God cannot lie, but we can. I'll tell you later why Rod was so mistaken.

For Christmas that year, Louis and I went to the local Cadillac dealer, where I bought him a brand new silver Cadillac, I never said a word, I watched, as Louis talked to the salesman and worked out the deal, he is wise beyond his years, and I really do have a parental love and pride for him. We had originally gone to the same local dealer that I always went to, but after standing around and looking for about thirty minutes, when no one ever came over to assist us, I told Louis that we should leave, I guess we didn't look like we were going to buy a car, needless to say, we never went there again, never judge a book by its cover, more often than not, you will misjudge.

I've watched Louis grow up, I actually do, partially feel that he's my son. I've watched him graduate from high school and go out into the workforce, I have seen this young man literally go from nothing to something. His tithe, is now the largest in the entire congregation, now mind you, this is the boy that used to put twenty-five cents in his tides envelope. I am also the one that married he and Carol, I christened both his sons, and have prayed for him without ceasing, Louis is the closest thing to a son I've ever had, and gladly, his parents understand this.

I have often tried to tell him, that church-folk will take advantage of you, and I am going to make a man out of him if it's the last thing that I do, I want him to depend solely on God, because man will let you down every time, God will never leave you, nor will he ever forsake you, it is just not in his nature to do this.

A new year has rolled around now, and not wanting to be too lenient on him, I myself, did something that I had to repent for, Louis had a check, that he had asked me to cash for him, instead of trading his old car in, he had sold it, and the gentleman that had purchased it from him, had given him a check drawn on an out of town credit union, but the check would take three days to clear, and Louis didn't have enough money in his account to cover it, and he needed it for the new car that he was purchasing that day, I actually told him, that I couldn't do it.

You wouldn't believe the way that God whipped me, all that night, I called Louis first thing that following morning, I told him that I was sorry, and how the Lord had dealt with me all that night, and to come over right then and I would gladly cash the check for him, thanks he said, but he had gotten it cashed already.

When someone misuses you or takes advantage of you, if you really are a child of God, don't worry about it, remember, I've already shared with you that the word of God will not return unto him void **(Isaiah 55:11)**.

Hebrews 10:30

"For we know him that hath said, Vengeance belongeth unto me, I will recompense, saith the Lord. And again, the Lord shall judge his people."

If and when God wants to get an individuals attention, he sometimes has to take him through some things, but fear not, God can repay an individual, in such a way, that many times, they will come back to you and beg your pardon, you see, many of the things that an individual may go through, its just because God has been dealing with them, to go and right some wrong that they have done, but out of their stubbornness or rebelliousness, they have simply refused, but God can out wait an individual. Many times when we try to fix it, we'll mess it up worst, than if we had just left it alone, but when you serve an awesome and almighty God, just stand back and see the salvation of the Lord.

I really did feel bad about not cashing the check, but it was part of Louis's first steps to learning how to be an independent man, and to not depend on anyone else aside from God, he never asked me for another favor after that, I was the one always needing him, and he was always there for me, never one to hold any malice, or grudges. Well, you might ask, if I really felt bad, why take it this far, because, I'm church-folk, and

"CHURCH-FOLK SOME MESSED-UP FOLK"

In March, of that following year, I told Louis that we needed to go back to the dealership, you see unbeknownst to him, the salesman there, had been calling me for over two months, trying to persuade me to buy a brand new limousine that they had in stock, and for some reason it just wasn't selling. Louis came to my apartment and picked me up, and off we went to the automobile dealer.

When we got there, Louis treated me like I was his real father, he explained to me, that he thought it cost too much, that it was not practical, you see I never sat in the backseat, and he reminded me of this, I told him that the reason I never sat in the backseat was because I always wanted to see where I was going, I also told him that I had always wanted a black limousine, it just makes you feel important I said, that day we left the dealership headed home in a brand new, shiny black, Cadillac limousine, I was in heaven. Louis also talked them down another $5000.

The next month, someone came to me after morning services one Sunday, and told me that Louis had put Carol out, and that she was living at home with her parents, I called Louis into my office and asked him if that was true, and he said that it was, I told him that he had better go and get her, and take her back home right then, and he did just that. I only wanted what was best for them, and the timing was all wrong. As it stands, life is going to throw him enough curve balls as it is, and he doesn't need marital problems to compound it, God knows what each and every one of us are going through, wait on him.

I have a secretary right now named Gladys Gunn, that Louis and Carol are very fond of, and they think, that the feelings are mutual, occasionally they all go out to dinner together, she sometimes invites them over to her house, and at times they invite her over to theirs.

Louis was over to my house one day, when I sat him down and gave him a good talking to, I told him, that he was not to trust Gladys, I also told him that she did not care very much for him, he was thoroughly shocked, and I believe if it had been anyone else, he might have come right out and called me a liar.

From that day on, he was much more careful, and watchful of her. Gladys is looking for power, prestige and position, and she knows, that being the wife of a Bishop she would have them all. I also told Louis, that if my last wife had not treated me so badly, that I honestly would have let Gladys talk me into marrying her, but after that last wife, I made the Lord a promise, that once he got me out of that marriage, I would never marry again, and I was determined not to.

Louis had no way of knowing the things that Gladys was saying to me about him, every opportunity that presented itself, she would bad mouth him to me, she would tell me that he didn't do anything for me that she couldn't do, and that we really didn't need him around, she was always very careful, to make it a point, to come over when Louis wasn't there. She didn't realize the parental love that I had for him. Didn't I tell you

"CHURCH-FOLK SOME MESSED-UP FOLK"

The majority of the time, she would tell me when she was coming over, and it was always to do something for me, anytime I knew that she was coming though, I would tell Louis to take some money out, and leave it on the table for her, I didn't want anyone to feel that I owed them anything. All of my life, I had paid my own way, and I still felt a need to do this.

The only reason that I had married before anyway, was that the founder of our great organization, who had founded it in the early 1900's, had also stipulated in the church by-laws, that a Bishop must be married, therefore when the founders health had began to rapidly deteriorate, seeing as though I had came along with him in the early days of the church, I knew, that if I was to ever be ordained as a Bishop, it would have to be before he died, because there were certain individuals in place now, that if I wasn't a Bishop when the founder died, I never would become one.

For this reason, and this reason alone, in 1972, I asked one of the single women in the church to marry me, although she was not my first choice, she accepted, we were married the following month, and that following year, I was ordained a Bishop. Six months later, our church founder died, and three years after that my marriage ended, why, because we were church-folk, and

"CHURCH-FOLK SOME MESSED-UP FOLK"

The founder had left specific instructions on how the church was to be ran, the governing board, consisting of seven Bishops, an odd number for voting purposes, there was:

Bishop Jett Black (our founder)
Bishop Skyy Blue
Bishop Bobo Brown
Bishop Invy Green
Bishop Varri Bright
Bishop Harry Gray
And myself,
Bishop Puir White.

Upon the death of our great founder, we had unanimously voted another Bishop in, that had been with us over the last ten years, he had come her from Africa, his name was,

Bishop Nattu Worthy

This rounded off our new governing board, and in accordance with instructions given by the founder, Bishop Black, prior to his death, each would take two year terms, being in charge, each being given the respected title of the Chief Disciple. The first one to take charge would be Bishop Bright, who had been the founding Bishop's assistant, needless to say, pride crept in, and the first one at the helm refused to step down after his two year term, why, because he was church-folk, and

"CHURCH-FOLK SOME MESSED-UP FOLK"

Therefore the rest of the Bishops, including myself, not wanting to stir up too much controversy in the church, we all conceded, and allowed him continue as the Chief Disciple, that was our first mistake, he had counted on this.

Make no truce with sin, for the bible says,

1st John, 5:17

"All unrighteousness is sin: and there is a sin not unto death."

Many of us have compromised our ways, right into hell, we have become a people that are far too passive,

1st Corinthians 5:6

"Your glorying is not good. Know ye not that a little leaven leaveneth the whole lump?"

Don't let the devil get his foot in the door, we must learn how to deal with sin, and sinful people, too many of us see, allow, and participate in things that we ought not to, we must stop sin in its tracks, the moment it reaches our door. The greed for and the love of money, have been a great downfall, to a countless number of individuals.

All of us Bishops knew, that the founding Bishop, whom we referred to as the Chief Disciple, was quite well off, but what we saw upon his death, we were really unprepared for, he had a vault in his office, with checks and envelopes stuffed with cash, some dating back about forty years, greed has no eyes, it will take hold of whomever allows it to, The integrity of our great organization was never the same once the founder died.

Often, I would try to emphasize to Louis, on every occasion when possible, don't be so quick to do anything for money, the consequences are not always worth it, my prayer for this young man, is that the Lord will abundantly bless him and that he would not lack financially.

That summer I told Louis that we should all go on vacation, I said that we should all go to that big state amusement park that I had heard so much about.

Louis called and reserved us two suites, right across from the park. He told me that he would pick me up in his car, and he told me what time to be ready, I told him that we were riding in style, in my car, so they picked me up in the limousine, and off we headed to the amusement park. One of the things that most people noticed about he and Carol, was that their boys were two of the most well behaved children, that you could ever come into contact with, even in the car, they traveled well, most of the time, I'd be looking in the back seat to see if they were asleep, they never were.

Once we got to the hotel and checked in, we all had dinner, and relaxed for the most part that evening. The next morning, here they all come, Louis, Carol, Junior and Byron, knocking on my door, he said that they had come to take me to breakfast before we all went to the amusement park, I told him, man you must be crazy, what would I look like going to an amusement park, as old as I am, but it was your idea Bishop he said, I know I said, but when we left home, I had no intention on going to that park, I just wanted to bring you, Carol and the children, so you all could enjoy yourselves, I gave him a thousand dollars and told him to get out of here.

I told them that I would eat downstairs in the restaurant, and I did just that, I also never left the hotel, the whole time we were there. They all thanked me, and told me that they had all had a wonderful time.

One of the great controversies in the church is, concerning receiving the gift of the Holy Ghost, and the gift of speaking with other tongues, and this is something that Louis questions me about all of the time, the best analogy that I told him that I could give him was, that when you go into a store to buy a pair of shoes, what do you tell the store clerk that you would like to buy, well Louis said, you tell him just that, that you'd like to buy a pair of shoes, well I said, why don't you tell him that you'd like to buy a pair of tongues, if you buy the shoes Louis said, the tongues are a part of them, just as with the Holy Ghost I explained, if you get the Holy Ghost, the tongues are there, and if and when needed they will exhibit themselves, as the spirit of God gives the utterance.

We must be most careful in this area, for the way some teach, if you have deaf and dumb loved ones, there is no possibility of them ever being filled with the Holy Ghost, the mind is a very powerful thing, and I have seen so many, that have been taught in error.

The world has now manufactured its own set of tongues, and that's just what I mean, manufactured, some of the lifestyles, that so called Christians lead today, is enough to make you wonder if they know what the word Christian really means, it means Christ like, and if you're not willing to live a life pleasing to God, Christian is a name that we should not wear, speaking in tongues is good, but the real evidence of the Holy Ghost, is a changed life, when the spirit of Christ resides in an individual, he simply cannot continue to do the things that he used to do, when one has genuinely received the gift of God, it will manifest itself in the love that he shows for his fellow man, in the very manner in which he now conducts himself, the very tone of his voice will display it, when one has really received the bread of life, all who come into his presence will know that something has changed, and that there is a reality in serving the true and living God.

Some of the things that I personally, have seen some people do, and that I personally, have heard some people say, after they have spoken in tongues, lets me know that they have not really come into the saving knowledge of Jesus Christ, singing and shouting is all right, but God is looking for changed lives to back up these lofty testimonies that we share.

Romans 13:11

"And that, knowing the time, that now it is high time to awake out of sleep: for now is our salvation nearer than when we believed."

I have seen so much corruption in my lifetime, in and out of the church, that if Jesus came back right now, it would not be too soon for me, neither would it surprise me, we are truly living in the last days, we can almost stop looking for his eminent return, and start listening for it, he is coming back, even though,

"CHURCH-FOLK SOME MESSED-UP FOLK"

I've got more money owed to me right now, than I can count, mostly by church-folk, I have told Louis, that I honestly believe, many of these church-folk have borrowed money from me, hoping that I'll die and they won't have to pay it back to me, this in spite of the fact that I give more money away every year, than many people earn. Many of the very ones waiting for my demise, have passed on themselves with my money. I am continually telling Louis, don't let people do this same thing to you, but he's too soft in that area, one day, trust me he'll learn, or he'll be broke.

Later that year, I went to see my attorney, I told him that I wanted to have my will drawn up, up until this time I had never given it much thought, because up until now, I really didn't care where my money went, I had always figured I'd just let everybody fight over it. Things had changed now, and I cared too much for Louis to not reward him for his kindness to me, I had my attorney name Louis, as my executor, and sole beneficiary, he deserves it I said, I have never had anyone who looked out for me the way that he does, neither have I ever been the pastor of a church, where I saw an individual with such a giving heart.

I have often told Louis how I came up, like a slave, coming out of Egypt, many days I told him, I didn't know where my next meal was coming from, and I had gone to bed hungry, a many nights, many nights I didn't have a bed to go to, I slept outdoors, many times, no one wanted to be bothered with me, not even family. How many of you know, that when you don't have anything, or any money, and can't do anything for them, many folks don't want to be bothered with you, I also told him that I've gone through a big portion of my life, feeling like I've had to buy most people. I just wanted to make sure that Louis had it a lot better than I did, and I pray that God will continue to give him wisdom in the area of finances also.

I am also very fond of Louis's parents, and I know that he will always be there for them, they've had a very rough life, and have never had much, but it was his mother, who has held that family together, through thick and thin, mostly thin. Most women would have never put up with what she has had to endure, Louis was their youngest child, so I had been there the majority of his lifetime, his mother Edith, was truly the woman spoken of in **Proverbs 31**, she had been one of the most faithful members of the church, since the time that I had first arrived there, I had seen such sincerity, humility and love in her, and I had so often thought, how could a righteous God continue to let her endure such abuse, as that being administered by her husband Al, who from the time I had arrived there, I had never seen him sober, had never heard of him having a job, and the only time he ever came to church, was in a drunken stupor, to disrupt service, and to make her leave with him.

I sat there, and I watched her for many many years, I often prayed for her and her children, and I thought to myself, God would not allow her to continue to go through this. I had often thought to myself, if anything would ever happen to Al, this is the kind of woman that I would like for my wife, although neither of us, have ever said one word to the other out of place, and its not like I was sitting around waiting on something to happen, but no one can live too long, that continues living that kind of lifestyle, he wasn't your ordinary alcoholic, he was a sloppy, seven day a week drunk.

But after much thought, and many years had gone by, I said to the Elders at the church, if we really believe in the God that we preach about, we should be able to pray Al Timm's through. So in September of 1974, we began a special prayer and fasting service at the church.

We decided to go over to their house one night to have an old fashioned prayer meeting, they were living in the housing projects at that time, and that night, the power of God came down in a mighty way, I have seen change come into the lives of individuals before, but that night God moved mountains for the entire Timm's family, that night Al Timms, became Brother Al Timms.

That night the Lord delivered him from alcohol, cigarettes, cursing, lying and adultery, all at once, and to this day, I have experienced this change firsthand, this was no temporary fix. Since that night, Brother Timms has never been a problem in the church, at home, or anywhere else for that matter, he got a job that following month, and has been gainfully employed every since, he has also been one of the most faithful members, and generous financial supporters of the church since that time, this is what prayer meetings are supposed to be all about.

To anyone who may be wondering, he's still the same God, and yes God still moves mountains in the lives of his people.

2nd Timothy 2:3

"Thou therefore endure hardness, as a good soldier of Jesus Christ."

When you think about someone enduring hardness as a good soldier, she has weathered the storm more gracefully, than anyone else that I have ever seen in all my years in the ministry, myself included. I would often wonder why a person with such a beautiful spirit, could have been dealt such a messed up hand in life, but brother Al is working double time, to try and be everything in a man, that a woman of Edith's caliper deserves.

I do believe as some do, in generational curses, and things that can come down through family lines, and mark a person, but for the most part, these are conscious choices that we make as individuals, and grab hold of, many times because we are not willing to stand up and take responsibility. Many times because of things that have happened in our lives, that are just so devastating that we feel we just really can't talk about, there's not a friend like the lowly Jesus, he knows all of our troubles, he is willing to aid all who come to him with their heavy burdens, that are more than they themselves can bear, God ever cares for his own.

Al and Edith Timms had not been brought up in the fear and admonition of God, they had not been brought up with a lot of family values necessary to maintain a healthy relationship. A big part of Al's problem, was that he was the youngest of twenty-four children, and being the youngest he had been allowed to shirk a lot of the responsibility that normally fell to a young man his age.

Al had been born into a unique blended family, his mother Betty, had eleven children, and her husband William died, her neighbor Elgin and his wife Elizabeth, had twelve children, and Elizabeth died, that's when Betty and Elgin got married, and gave birth to Louis, who now came into a family with twenty-three half brothers and sisters all under the age of sixteen, and boy did they spoil him. He never had to do a thing for himself, he never had chores at home to do, he was never given any responsibility, and as he grew older, that didn't change, this all carried over into his adult life, you see many of the things that we do, are learned over a period of time, and in much the same way, they have to be unlearned.

You can understand and relate to why Al was the way that he was, but to understand and relate to all of an individuals idiosyncrasies, still does not make them acceptable.

Edith on the other hand was just the opposite, she was the firstborn in a family of fourteen, and had always been the one to take responsibility, it was always her job, to see to it, that the house was clean, the dinner was cooked, and that the younger children were bathed, dressed and fed, so you see, when you put two people like that together, you're almost asking for disaster.

But God, anytime you factor God into the equation, you can take the problems and reverses of life, and all will be made smooth sailing. Through many dangers, toils and snares, God had already brought them, many times they didn't know how they were going to make it, but with God's help, they made it.

Any one can go through something, when they can see that proverbial light at the end of the tunnel, but just how long do you wait for a change to come, just how much do you endure in the interim. For twenty six years, Edith had lived below the poverty level, was evicted from five different places of residence. At twenty-one years old, she already had five children. She had no marketable skills, no one to turn to for help or for consolation, they never stayed in any one place, longer than eight months. One night a neighbor invited her to a revival that her church was having, Edith attended, and it was truly, the best night of her life, and even though she did not immediately begin attending church, something got a hold of her, and I didn't matter what she did or where she went, she couldn't get that night out of her mind.

The following year, they headed north, following some of Al's family members, by now there were six children, and they all moved in with some of Al's family members for about seven months, while applying for welfare and looking for housing of their own.

When they did finally find a place of their own to move into, there was a little Pentecostal church on the corner, and as she passed by and heard the service going on one night, Edith thought about the night that she had gone to that old time revival, the next Sunday she went to visit that little church, she joined, and from that day on she has been walking with Jesus every since. After that, life wasn't always easy, but she never looked back, always had a smile or a kind word, God saved her, she received the gift of the Holy Ghost, and from that day on, she has been a blessing to everyone that she has come into contact with, because she has the real love of Jesus, down in her heart.

For years the Timm's family struggled, never having much, but she said, she had given her life to Christ, and that it was now his job to take care of them, and although it might not always be the nicest of places, they always had a place to stay, and food to eat.

Romans 8:18

"For I reckon that the sufferings of this present time are not worthy to be compared with the glory which shall be revealed in us."

If there's one point I'd really like to convey here, it is that God pays the highest price, we must remember that this life is only temporary, and do we really want to forfeit eternity, by being so wrapped up with the cares of this world, God promised the believer one thing, that is eternal life, what ever we have to go through in this short time span called life, will pale in comparison to the glory which shall be revealed in us, when we are eternally in God's presence, to gain the whole world, and lose out with God, is it really worth it.

Although the Timm's came up north with only six children, more were born once they arrived here, and the children, I don't know if it was just their children, or all children in general, but they were more understanding, and grateful for what they had, than the children are today. Edith brought them up in the fear and admonition of the Lord, they were never complainers, like some of the children I have seen, and they all, had a genuine love for their mother, don't misunderstand me, they loved their father also, but it was just different with Momma.

She had a real mothers love also, and one of the important things that she had always done, was kept them always before the Lord in prayer, morning and night, how many of you know, that even when you do your very best, things don't always seem to work out the way you would like for them to, however, we must still do our part, because right, is always the right thing to do, its in God's word, and God is always on the side of right, just trust him, if you love him and keep his commandments, you will always be victorious, even in death, think about this, the absolute worst thing that can happen to any of us is that we could be put to death, if we die in Christ, we will live again, let me rephrase that, the absolute worst thing that can happen to any of us, is that we die, and not know God in the free pardon of our sins.

Many things went on in Louis's life that year, but the one thing that I cannot emphasize enough is, that in our lives, most of us will never know on this side of the grave, the things, rather the powers that are at work behind the scenes, in the life of the true child of God,

Romans 8:28

"And we know that all things work together for good to them that love God, to them who are the called according to his purpose".

One night as Louis was driving home with a friend, he stopped at a green light, the friend asked him why was he stopping, Louis replied he didn't know, just then a car sped across in front of them, at ninety miles an hour, and if he hadn't stopped he would have certainly been hit, also we were on our way home from church one night, and the same exact thing happened, Gods angels are ever watching over us.

That same year, after eight years on his job, Louis missed his third day, he worked the third shift, and normally left the house about 11:00 P.M., that night, at about 10:15 P.M., as he was getting dressed for work, he felt nauseous, but he was determined that he was going to work anyway, he began to vomit, but still, he said that he was going to go to work anyway, he developed diarrhea to the point, that he became dehydrated and could barely stand up by himself, finally he decided to call in sick, this was the last day that he ever missed work, he normally had a very tough stomach, nothing had ever bothered him up to this point, however this night God was at work in Louis's life, as you'll all see later on.

Louis had another neighbor on the other side of him by the name of Maggie, who also worked the third shift, she and her fourteen year old son Jimmy, were the only two who lived there.

The morning after this bout with sickness, Maggie called him, she asked if everything was alright, she said that when she had gotten in that morning, Jimmy had told her, that he had been looking out their back window the night before, and had seen someone standing on the side of Louis's garage, as if they were waiting for him to come out, Louis explained to her that he had been very sick the night before, and had not gone to work, this story we'll conclude later.

There was also the time that Louis, and Bernardo the friend that he worked with, and rode together with, were on there way home from working the third shift, and Louis had often kidded Bernardo about the fact, that every single time they had gotten into the car, when it was Louis's week to drive, that Bernardo had gone to sleep before they were a quarter of the way home, this particular morning was no different, except Louis went to sleep also, yes while he was driving, and upon hearing an audible voice, he awakened to find the front end of his car, right under the back-end of an eighteen wheeler, this was before the law mandated that trucks have crash bars installed, his car was about two inches away from touching the trucks rear wheels, he looked over at Bernardo, who was still asleep, and never even knew what had happened, until Louis told him the next morning.

Louis had had a very long friendship with Bernardo, they had gone to school together every since they were ten years old, and after graduation, began working together at eighteen years old. This too shows the sovereignty of God, when Louis had first applied for the job, he didn't even know that Bernardo worked there, once all the paperwork was done and the physical was taken and passed, and a starting date was determined, he went over to Bernardo's house, to tell him about it, you see Bernardo had been enrolled in the local community college, and when Louis had last talked to him, as far as he knew, his friend was still enrolled at the college.

When Louis arrived to tell him about his new job, Bernardo told Louis that he wouldn't believe it, but he said college just wasn't for him, and that just the month before, he had dropped out of college and accepted a job at the same company. After this, the two of them began riding together, and for the first three years they did this. So where does the sovereignty of God come into play at, three months after Louis started, he got fired, but thanks to Bernardo, his job was spared.

The job, and how he came about getting it also displays the sovereignty of God, you see this was a company that you just didn't get hired into, that is without knowing someone, and it was two years before Louis found out himself, how even he had gotten the job.

Louis's youngest two sisters had filled out job applications and applied for a couple of general positions at this company, when I refer to Louis two youngest sisters, he has five sisters, these are the youngest of the five girls, anyway after applying, they told Louis that he should also apply, he wasn't really interested though, because he had just started a job five months earlier, and the favor of God had already displayed itself there, he was such a good and faithful worker, that his superiors there told him, that if he had anyone that he could recommend, they would hire them on the spot, because of his faithfulness, his brother, two friends, and three cousins, were also hired into that company, and this was all within that five month period.

Nevertheless at his sisters urging, Louis did eventually go and apply at the company that they had told him about, he was hired, and neither of them were ever called. When he left his old job, they noted in his employee file, that if he ever needed to return, he always had a job there.

So where does the sovereignty of God come into play at in getting this new job, two years after starting this job, Louis received his medical coverage cards, the job only offered two choices at the time, and the cards that Louis had received were not for the medical coverage that he knew that he had chosen, upon calling the Human Resources office, Louis learned from the very same individual there that had originally hired him, that when he was hired, there was another Louis Timms, that had been hired that very same day, well Louis inquired, shouldn't you all have at least noticed the birthdays, that's the irony of it all said this individual, both of you have the exact same birthday, he told Louis that he was to send the hospital cards back, inter-office mail, and that he would handle it from there.

You see these were the other Louis's cards, this was the medical coverage that he had chosen. This was the Louis that had known someone at the company, the Louis that someone else had put in a good word for, and the director of Human Resources, told my Louis that he just thought it would be a topic of discussion, once the two of them had met each other, well they never did meet, the other Louis did not work out, and right after that mix-up, he was let go.

Now isn't that just like the God we serve, before Louis was formed in his mothers womb, God knew him, and had already chosen his name,

Jeremiah 1:5

"Before I formed thee in the belly I knew thee: and before thou camest forth out of the womb I sanctified thee, and I ordained thee a prophet unto the nations."

Now where would Louis be, if his name had been anything other than, Louis Timms, God only knows.

The true child of God cannot help but be blessed, and likewise, to be a blessing to someone else in return, but we cannot play church, no one may know it, but you and God, isn't that enough, just knowing that he, has an all seeing eye, should be enough in and of itself, to make us want to live a holy and righteous life, not out of fear, but out of reverence for who he is, and for what he has done for each and everyone of us.

It sorely disturbs me, when I hear an individual say that God hasn't done anything for them, the fact that they are here in the land of the living, that in and of itself is a blessing. Church-folk might not say that God hasn't done anything for them, but they live like it, of the many people that you will come into contact with in your lifetime, many will leave an indelible influence on you, and likewise you on them, how do we want to be remembered as one who claims to be a child of God, the life that we live, and the service that we give, we should do all things, wanting the world to see Jesus in our lives.

How have you lived your life, it really doesn't matter to me, but it does matter to God, and it should matter to you, all an individual is doing while observing your lifestyle, is forming an opinion of you, its true that only God knows the heart, but when you're trying to serve God half-heartedly, you're not serving him at all, you're appeasing yourself with that I'm just as good as anybody else mentality, God is not looking for religious nuts, he is and always has been looking for spiritual fruit.

When it comes right down to it, your relationship with God, is not about anybody else anyway, the bible says that you, are to save yourselves;

Acts 2:40

"And with many other words did he testify and exhort, saying, Save yourselves from this untoward generation."

When we can continue to go to church, week after week after week, and the word of God does nothing to change an individuals heart and life, it is a very easy thing to become desensitized to the word of God, thus rendering his word ineffective, not only in our own lives, but also in the lives of those observing us.

We must at all cost guard or hearts, against anything that would turn our hearts from the true and living God. He gave his all for us, should we not in turn, give our all to him.

3

"SOME FINANCIAL INFORMATION"

Malachi 3:8

"Will a man rob God?, Yet ye have robbed me, but ye say, wherein have we robbed thee?, In tithes and offerings."

Do you really believe, that as individuals, we should give God a tenth of our earnings. Many believe that its too much of a sacrifice, and that they simply could not make ends meet, trying to live on the other ninety percent. I dare you to give God his tenth, and see won't he make the ninety percent, go farther than the one hundred percent. There's a good chance, that if you can't live on the ninety percent, you're struggling with the one hundred percent anyway.

Another great controversy in the church, is tithes and offerings. Statistically it has been shown, that thirty-five percent of the people that make up most of our congregations, put little, if any money at all in the church, of the sixty-five percent of the remaining people, seven percent, actually do give at least a tenth of their income, so what do the other fifty-eight percent give?, pretty much whatever they feel like giving.

Unfortunately this is a sign of the spiritual atmosphere in most of our churches today, seven percent, are actually trying to serve God with all of their heart, mind and soul, to the best of their ability, thirty five percent are callous, dry and cold, and most of them know it, and they don't care, one way or the other, if you know it, or what you think about them, the other fifty-eight percent are trying to serve God to some extent, knowing that they're not giving it their all in all, but they have the, that's good enough mentality.

My question then is this, the same as a little child asked, as he and his parents were preparing to leave the local restaurant that they had been dining at, as the father was so carefully figuring out what the tip should be, the child asked, Daddy, why is it that we give God ten percent, but we give the waitress fifteen percent, out of the mouth of babes, what perception, this should give us all something to think about, shouldn't it.

For the seven percent, who do give a tenth, the great controversy lies herein, do you tithe on your net or your gross. Well in 1987, Louis heard a message on tithing that changed him from that moment on, and as he sat there, the point that the preacher was trying to convey to the listener was this, that if you're already trying to do the right thing by paying your tithes, ask God to reveal his will to you in this area of your life, that night the minister challenged his listening audience, by telling them to stretch out on God concerning this, and whether you pay a tenth on the net, or on the gross, could ultimately be determined by this one factor, and this one factor alone, that determining factor would be that the choice was yours, you pay your tithes on your net or your gross, based solely on this factor, whether you wanted a net blessing, or a gross blessing from God.

Louis took the challenge that very night, he immediately began paying his tithes on his gross, and that very same year, the Lord blessed him mightily, and he went from driving a Mercedes, to driving a Rolls Royce. Now I'm not telling everyone to expect this from God, I'm simply saying that there are limitless possibilities with God, there is nothing wrong with prosperity, but Jesus himself said that the poor will be with you always.

One Sunday Louis called me to ask if it would be okay with me, if he picked me up for church that Sunday in his Rolls Royce, I told him that I didn't mind, now when he arrived, he got out to open the door for me, and I got in and off we went, I really enjoyed it, not the fact that I was riding in a Rolls Royce, what I enjoyed most, was that the steering wheel was on the right side of the vehicle, that was why he had gotten out to open the door for me, I was trying to get in the wrong door, now mind you, by this time I was already eighty something years old, and heading to church everyone was looking at us in the car, and I looked and felt like I was the one driving.

Many individuals felt that it was quite vain of Louis to drive a Rolls Royce, but as a sixteen year old young man, he had worked as a janitor in a clothing store, there was an Art Gallery next door to it. One day as he was cleaning near the front window of the clothing store, he saw a big, white, 1960, Rolls Royce, Silver Cloud II, pulling up and parking out front, as the driver backed into the parking space, and began to exit the vehicle, by this time Louis was already outside now, with his mouth open so wide, that she could have parked the car right in there.

A petite, one hundred pound, middle aged woman exited the vehicle, she noticed how Louis was admiring the vehicle, she was the one that ran the Art Gallery next door, and as she went in, she spoke to Louis, but he was in such awe, that he was speechless, he stayed outside and admired that car, for the next twenty minutes, he had never seen one up close before. Once he regained his faculties, he went into the Art Gallery and apologized to the woman, he struck up a friendship with her, her name was Ellen Snader.

It was Ellen, who had gotten Louis his first, full time job, after he graduated from high school. It was also Ellen, who instilled in a young man, brought up in the lap of poverty, the deep desire, to say to himself that one day, he was going to own a Rolls Royce, it was not so much vanity, it was more so, a young man fulfilling his childhood dreams.

How many of you know, that if and when a man's ways please the Lord, that the Lord can, and sometimes will give that man the very desires of his heart. We simply cannot half-step on God, the word of God is sharp, and it will find each and every one of us, wherever we are, or for that matter, wherever we are not.

Hebrews 4:12

"For the word of God is quick, and powerful, and sharper than any twoedged sword, piercing even to the dividing asunder of soul and spirit, and of the joints and marrow, and is a discerner of the thoughts and intents of the heart."

Another part of the big reason Louis turned out as well as he did, was an old proverb, that he carried with him in his heart, for the most part, his entire life, he had first heard it from his brother Rod, when he was only a child, it goes something like this:

"There was a wise owl, who sat in an oak
The more he heard, the less he spoke
The less he spoke, the more he heard
Louis chose to be, like that wise old bird"

I tell you this, to say that Louis, as a young man, was exposed to many evil influences, from the ages of about ten to fourteen years old, he was his fathers running buddy, and to see so much as a young child, can be a very devastating thing, his father was under the total control of Satan, therefore he really did not fully comprehend exactly what it was that he was doing.

Louis was a regular at bars, juke joints and after hour joints, in one of these places in particular, he fell in love with a song on the jukebox, the title of the song was "Stoop down baby, and let your daddy see", now at this time this was an "X" rated song, that teetered on the verge of pornography, there was always a number of filthy women in these places, that would do any and everything for a dollar, he even knew of certain indiscretions on his own fathers part.

This is the sort of thing, that doing a young persons formative years, will put illicit desires in them, these kinds of perversions will either draw you towards them, or drive you away from them, thanks be to God that Louis did not succumb to any of these pressures.

Back to that old proverb that Louis carried in his heart, he had purposed in his heart at twelve years old, that after observing so much that had gone on, that he would never do any of these filthy things that he saw go on in some of these vulgar places, he promised God that with his help, he would never live a riotous life, drink, smoke or use filthy language, God blessed him and until this day, at forty something years of age, he still, has never even drank a beer.

Louis cursed at someone once when he was about fourteen years old, and this thing disturbed him so badly, that he never even did that again. One of the things that Louis often told his father, was that he had helped him in life, more than he knew, you see his father Al, had often told him that he was sorry for not being a better father, and that he had often wished he had been there for Louis, as a father should have been, and that he had often wished that he had set a better example, not only for Louis, but for all the children.

What Louis told his father, was that there are positive role models, and negative role models, and that we must learn from both of them, and that the negative things that one encounters in his lifetime, must also be a valuable tool for teaching us, and Louis told his father, that it was these many negative influences, that had helped him avoid many of the pitfalls in life that would have otherwise swallowed him up, and that seeing and observing so much, helped him to live vicariously through his father, thus avoiding having to actually indulge in many of these sinful practices himself.

Louis was also very faithful when it came to his job, partly for this same reason, as a young man, Al had never been the sole provider for his family, he had never held onto a job for very long, therefore he had never become vested in a company, where at the appropriate age or with the given number of years, he would be able to draw some kind of retirement benefits, he was now fast approaching retirement age.

Matthew 5:45

"That ye may be the children of your father which is in heaven: for he maketh his sun to rise on the evil and on the good, and sendeth rain on the just and on the unjust."

Well bless God, at fifty five and fifty seven years of age, Louis found both parents the perfect jobs, at a local college, five minutes from their home, on the 10:00 P.M. to 6:00 A.M. shift, they both loved it, they said that they would get to work at 10:00 P.M., have the biggest portion of their work done by midnight, take it easy up until about 5:30 A.M., then wrap things up and prepare to leave, this took them right up through the next ten years, where they were both able to retire, with full benefits, we will elaborate on this a little later.

Do you really believe that there is a blessing in helping those out who are less fortunate than you are. From this point on in his life, Louis never had any financial problem, of the many other problems that may have plagued him, money was never one of them.

That year he also found some things that just did not add up with his wife Carol, money had began to disappear, he called the bank where their accounts were held, all to no avail, and there were nights that he'd be at work, and money would be withdrawn from ATM machines, as far as twenty-five miles away, and Carol always said she didn't know anything about it, only time would tell.

As a young man, Louis had been in the local chapter of the 4-H club, and he and the leaders of the club, who became a life long friend of the entire Timm's family, had grown up together, he had done very well for himself, he had gone away to college, became a lawyer, and had now opened up his own practice here in the city.

This was the friend, whom Louis had called to tell about some of the problems that he had been having with Carol, upon discussing certain pertinent issues, what this friend informed Louis of, was that it would be much cheaper, to try and work things out with Carol, if it were at all possible, because trying to pay alimony and child support for two children, would leave him with virtually nothing to live on for himself. It was at this point that Louis made it up in his mind, that he would try with all his might, to stay in this marriage, until Junior and Byron were at least eighteen years old, he also became much more aware of his surroundings.

I generally kept a briefcase full of money at my apartment, Louis did not like this and had been on me for years, to not keep such a large amount of cash at my home, because aside from the two of us, there were a few others who knew about this as well. I told Louis the latter part of that year, to call his father, and bring him and Carol up to my apartment. I had now began to feel my age creeping up on me, and I also knew that my faculties were not as sharp as they had been in the past, I told Louis that they could count the money and take the biggest portion, and deposit it into his bank account, to just leave five thousand dollars there for me.

It took them two and a half hours to count the money, but Louis told me he did not want to put the money in his account, for fear that I, or someone else might think that he was trying to use me, therefore he deposited it into my account.

The apartment I lived in was also a government subsidized apartment, and my bank statement went straight to the rental office, which at that time, Louis did not know. The next month I chewed him out good, I received my rent statement, and my rent had gone up four-hundred percent, I told him that I should whip him. Louis didn't mind this though, he said that the last thing he wanted was any impropriety to arise over my money.

As I have already said, Louis's father had become a very loyal and faithful member to the church, he had also been called into the ministry, and about two and a half years ago, I made him my assistant pastor, many of the other ministers had been asking for quite some time when would I be appointing one. For many years, one of the elders that I had come along with was my assistant, he had now been dead for three years, and I wasn't in any big hurry to replace him. There are far too many people take the office of a minister too lightly, just looking for a name or title, along with a seat in the pulpit. I had been praying about this, long and hard, and I truly felt that I was following the Lords leading in choosing Al Timms.

Louis's call into the ministry has also been revealed and confirmed, but he is quenching it, one thing about him, he certainly wants to let his calling and election be sure,

2 Peter 1:10

"Wherefore the rather, brethren, give diligence to make your calling and election sure: for if you do these things, ye shall never fail."

That following year was a pivotal year in Louis's life, due to the fact that his father Al had lacked holding a job any significant time as a young man, and thinking well ahead to the age of retirement, if he should live that long, Louis wanted to make sure that he qualified for some sort of pension. Louis's job requirement, as most companies at that time, required that you had to be employed by the company at least ten years to become vested in the company, his job was an extremely hard one there, and the position he held in the factory, required that he rotate all three shifts, and most weeks required that he also work six days, therefore he had made it up in his mind, that he didn't care how hard the job was, he would stay there at least ten years, so that he could become vested.

That year, he had an industrial accident on the job, I got the telephone call at 3:00 A.M., right after he arrived at the hospital, and I immediately began to pray, God blessed and he didn't even have to be admitted, they examined him, stitched him up and sent him home. After that he was off work for seven weeks, this was the longest period of time that he had ever gone not working, since he was twelve years old. His job put him on their workers compensation plan, and sent him a check every two weeks. During this seven week period, he also flew to Wichita Kansas, and bought his third Rolls Royce, it took him twenty three hours to drive it home, something that he promised me he'd never do again.

Louis had not been accustomed to being off work, so after six weeks, he called his physician, and asked that he be given permission to return to work. The physician asked him to come in for a consultation, and the following week, he was allowed to return to work. The fact that Louis had been a model employee, his job was also more than willing to work with him, they asked him if he would like to return to his old job, to which he responded no, therefore, they placed him in what he described as a nice cushiony job in the office, where after three promotions, his pay has more than doubled.

In addition to this, pertaining to the accident, the company also gave him a cash settlement, and sent him a check, every two weeks, for the next four years. In addition to all of that, because of the white collar position he now held, the desire to leave after ten years had now also subsided, he now worked a straight day shift job, five days a week. God works in a mysterious way, his wonders to perform.

Louis had also learned a valuable lesson about saving money, in his heart, what he had purposed was that he would save ten-thousand dollars a year, in addition to paying his tithe and offerings. Louis said that he knew what is was like to be poor, and that he knew what it was like to be broke, and that neither was any fun.

Louis would often counsel his family members, telling them that anyone that owns a house or a car, should have a hedge fund, something to fall back on, in case of an emergency. Statistics have shown that the average person is two paychecks away from being in poverty.

Louis did not want to be a part of this statistic, and he had sacrificed so much, for so long in his life, that he had now made it up in his mind, that anything he bought, he wanted to make sure he was able to keep it. He had seen too many people find out when it was too late, that it was harder to maintain things, than it was to obtain them.

Every year, I would have one of the younger Bishop's that I had mentored, come and run a one week revival for me, the majority of the time, it would be Bishop Gray, who only lived five hours away, aside from this, he would always ask me to allow him to do it anyway. Most years, he was the one that I would pay to take me to our annual meeting.

The biggest thing that I would always get on him about, was the fact that he was wearing my couch out, because whenever he would come into town, he would want to stay with me that whole week and sleep on my couch. I would always get on him, telling him that he shouldn't be so cheap, that he should want to stay at a nice hotel, that the church would even pay for it, for years he'd take the money, and still wear my couch out. Finally, just this last year, for the first time he decided to get a room at the hotel,

"CHURCH-FOLK SOME MESSED-UP FOLK"

It was also about this time, that Louis introduced me to a cousin of his, also named Rod, just as his brother, they had both been named after an uncle of theirs, anyway this cousin Rod, had come to church with Louis, during the revival that year that Bishop Gray was running, and during the open invitation to become a member at the end of the service, he had come forward and joined the church, he had previously gone to a church, where they would take you into the back room, and teach you how to speak in tongues.

Rod's parents had both tragically died a few years earlier, and the fact that he and Louis were less than a year apart, they had become quite close. I introduce him to you now, and will acquaint you with him in more detail later. Just remember his cousin Rod.

That year was also a pivotal year for me, that summer, I had attended our annual church meeting with Bishop Gray, when I returned home, I didn't seem to bounce back like I normally had, my age had now really began to show, and I had slowed down tremendously. I now needed and depended on Louis more than ever, it had become the norm, that he now left his job everyday and stopped by to check in on me, before he ever went home to his own family. Everyone involved, was quite understanding though.

It was also that same year, right around my birthday, that I had what I thought was a routine doctors appointment, I don't know about most people, but I have a terrible fear of going to doctors or dentists. This was early September and my appointment was at 1:00 P.M., Louis was at work, so instead of him taking off, whenever his father Al was available he would take me.

This particular time Al was the one that took me to the doctor, and the closer I got to the doctor, the more tense I had become, and by the time we actually got there, I was extremely nervous, and sweating profusely, and just as we were about to get out of the car, I had a panic attack, it was so severe that Al had to go inside and have them come out and take me straight into the emergency room, it was so severe that they all actually thought I had died, even Al.

Al actually went home and called Louis on his job and told him that I was dead, Louis was confused, he told his father that he thought it was just a routine check-up that I was going in for, well it was his father told him, but he said he didn't know what had gone wrong, but he was there, and that there was no way that I could have pulled through. Al was so certain that I was dead, that he had even taken my glasses and clothes home with him.

Louis told his father that he would leave work and head straight to the hospital, and he asked him if he would meet him there with my belongings, and Al said that he would. Well I had not died, the entire staff of doctors had worked on me extensively and brought me back around, they could not explain exactly what had happened, but for a man my age, I was doing as well as could be expected under the circumstances.

When Louis arrived he came into the room to see me, Bishop, he whispered, yeah son, I said, How are you he asked, I don't know I answered, about that time his father Al also arrived, he went out into the hallway and talked to him for a few minutes, and then the two of them came back in, and Louis put my glasses on me, that was a pretty rough one I told him, I also told him that I was tired of just about everything, of being old, of being sick and of being tired.

One of the things that I had always done, was to give Louis my briefcase, whenever I knew that I was going to be admitted into the hospital, I had not given it to him this time, because this was just supposed to be an outpatient visit, I now knew that I would be there a while, so I told him to go and get it, and to keep it at his house until I got out.

Because my age had now caught up with me, most of the time I now traveled in a wheelchair. Louis now had to come up to my apartment and get me whenever we had to go somewhere, and likewise when we returned, he had to take me back up to my apartment, therefore Louis had the only key to my door, I didn't have a key to my own apartment. Right or wrong, I loved my money and Louis knew this, therefore he assured me that he would go and get it. That night, I began to wonder if I ever would see my apartment again.

That evening, after leaving the hospital, he headed up to my apartment, when Louis arrived there it was kind of late, he could sense in his spirit that something was wrong, he went and looked in the place that he knew I normally kept the briefcase, and it was gone, the Lord immediately revealed to him who had taken it, not only was my briefcase gone, but so was all my jewelry and my pistol, that's right I said my pistol, so Louis called the police, they were there in no time, now mind you, Louis had the only key.

Upon questioning him, Louis told the authorities who had done it, they asked him how he knew this, now he couldn't very well tell them, because the Lord told me, now could he, He told them that he was the only one that had a key, and that the only other person that could have come in, would either be security, or someone that security had let in, therefore the officers called security up to the apartment, and sure enough they had a log, and they had been told that the Bishop had died, and they allowed his brother and sister to come in and pick up a few of his personal belongings.

Guess what, I didn't have a brother or a sister. As many of you well know, folks will signify around, trying to find out and get in your business, even when it doesn't pertain to them in any way at all, how many of you know, that if it doesn't involve you, you should stay out, and shut up, there are only two occasions where you should comment on another persons business, one is when they ask for your input, the other is when it is clearly a matter of life and death, if it doesn't concern you, at all cost, mind your own business.

Well at the hospital that evening, there just happened to be one of the church members employed there, who also thought that she had overheard someone say that I had died, and had taken it upon herself, to have someone from church go along with her, up to my apartment and concoct this lie. Now isn't

"CHURCH-FOLK SOME MESSED-UP FOLK"

Louis gave the officers the name and telephone number of this individual, the officers were told by her, that she only had some of my belongings, her accomplice had the rest, the officers told her to get in touch with her accomplice, and that the two of them could either bring it back, or the officers told them, that they would come and get it.

After about an hour passed, the two of them came ringing the buzzer, as one of the officers opened the door, they handed him the briefcase, along with the other goods. Louis was asked if he wanted to press charges, to which he responded no, I told him that he should have, they were both visibly upset with Louis. The next day Louis came to the hospital to see me, and he told me that someone had gone into the apartment and stolen my briefcase, I told him that he was the only one with a key, and that he had better be a man and handle his business, find out who took it and get it back, that's when he told me, that he had already gotten it back, along with telling me who had taken it.

I prayed about this situation, you see I was ready to give up and die, but this gave me a renewed will to live, just thinking that someone could do this to me, I asked the Lord to let me get better, and be able to get out of the hospital, at least long enough to tend to some unfinished business, and the Lord answered my prayer.

You see Louis was only in his twenties, and these individuals thought that they could run over him, or take advantage of him, and they were thoroughly shocked, that first of all he would even call the police on them, Louis was nobody's fool, maybe a little to soft-hearted at times, but nobody's fool, and it wasn't just him, what about my wishes, its these kind of things, that over time, will begin to eat away at an individual, and cause their hearts to become hardened.

I was released from the hospital three days later, and I couldn't wait, to meet with both of these individuals, and I did, separately, and I let go with a tirade of anger, that normally would have been shameful for a Bishop to display, but I let them know that when you try to take advantage of Louis, you're also trying to take advantage of me, and that he was only following my orders. Needless to say, Louis never had another problem with either of these individuals, at least not as long as I was alive and they feared the consequences.

I had given both these individuals money, on multiple occasions, and now to steal from me, basically that's what it was, and I felt that this was a slap in the face. Louis told them, that they knew he was the only one with a key, so why hadn't they called him, they said that they just weren't thinking, that in itself is a lie, they thought about it long and hard, and they knew exactly what they were doing. What would have been wrong with just saying, forgive me, I was wrong.

What I had learned, early in life, was that we must always remember the three "R's", they are, first of all, Respect for yourself, second is, Respect others, and lastly, Responsibility for all of our own actions, because good or bad, they do come with consequences.

Too many of us want to dance all around an issue, instead of just facing it head on, to ignore a problem, will not make it disappear, to give a smug answer, or tell someone exactly what they want to hear, will not erase it either. Respect is not deserved, it is something that must be earned, and many times an individual will ask you something, knowing the answer, only wanting to test your character, and in failing these tests, you have also risked your integrity, even if man doesn't catch you, you and God know what the real deal is.

After Adam and Eve had blown it, and God called out unto them:

Genesis 3:9

"And the Lord God called unto Adam, and said unto him, Where art thou?"

God didn't ask Adam where he was because he didn't know, he was giving Adam a chance to confess, and become reconciled with him, before it was too late.

In Exodus 2:11-14

"And it came to pass in those days, when Moses was a grown man, he went out to see his brothers, to see the burdens they were under, and he saw an Egyptian beating up one of his Hebrew brothers. He looked to the left ant to the right, and when he saw that there was no one around, he killed the Egyptian, and buried him in the sand. So he went out the next day, and two Hebrews were fighting each other, and Moses said to the one that was in the wrong, why are you fighting your brother? The Hebrew in question said, who made you a judge over us, do you intend to kill me, as you killed that Egyptian on yesterday? In shock, Moses feared, and said surely this thing is known."

Moses may have looked left and right, but he didn't look up, where an all seeing God, was looking down. Moses was forty years old during this time, after this, he ran from Egypt, to the land of Midian, where he stayed for another forty years, only to go back to Egypt afterwards, to face what he had left behind. You cannot run from your problems or your responsibilities, you must face up to whatever it is that befalls you, you can face it now, or you can face it later, the choice is yours.

Whatever you do, do not covet another mans worldly goods,

1st Timothy 6:10

"For the love of money is the root of all evil: which while some coveted after, they have erred from the faith, and pierced themselves through with many sorrows."

In doing this you allow the devil to get his foot into a door, that may otherwise have been shut to him. What God has for you, it is for you, and it doesn't matter who doesn't want to see you with it, if God is for you, he's more than the whole world against you. Jealousy, envy, covetousness, malice and all such as these, are as cruel as the grave, likewise, if God doesn't want you to have something, I don't care how you try to get it, or who tries to give it to you, you will never have it, or achieve it, there are those that spend their whole lives chasing this worlds vain riches, always to find that their just a step behind.

As I grow older, I've learned more of what the preacher meant in

Ecclesiastes 1:2

"Vanity of vanities, saith the Preacher, vanity of vanities; all is vanity."

Money tends to lose its value, when your health is failing, and what really matters most in a mans life, is the friendships that he has made, and the relationships that he has formed, beginning, with a right relationship with God, because it's only what we do for him, that will last or count anyway. Sure we've all made our share of mistakes, but we must learn from them, and we must not let them stunt our growth, in the end, they will make us better people, if we would only realize, that our trials only come to make us strong.

I feel that the lights of life are dimming for me now. I am now a shadow of the man that I used to be, Louis and I were out once, and I told him that in my mind, I could vividly remember the things that I had done as a ten year old boy, I told him that in my mind, I thought that I could run and jump up and do a somersault, but in my body, thank God I knew differently, I told him that I now felt like the little engine that thought it could.

I had always been very fussy, I now told Louis that I was sorry, and that I had hoped he had never paid me any mind in this respect. Sometimes as we get older, we become bitter and angry, we lash out at those that are closest to us, sometimes we are slightly jealous, that they still have youth on their side, beware, it is fleeting, and I often wonder where the years went, it seems that they had started skipping by twos, and then by fives.

4

"THE SUN IS GOING DOWN"

Philippians 1:21-24

"For me to live is Christ, and to die is gain. But if I live in the flesh, this is the fruit of my labor: yet what I shall choose I know not. For I am in a straight betwixt two, having a desire to depart, and to be with Christ, which is far better: Nevertheless to abide in the flesh is more needful for you."

1st Peter 4:7

"But the end of all things is at hand: be ye therefore sober, and watch unto prayer."

I had grown very weary of life, and I felt that my race had been run. My biggest fear now, was that the church, and the son, that I had loved and nurtured, would be eaten up by vultures, figuratively speaking of course.

I rarely get out of the apartment now, I no longer even go out to our midweek services any more, and now just going to Sunday morning services, pretty much wears me out. Bishop Brown came into town to see me today, he's been in the organization almost as long as I have, we had a nice long visit, I also told him about someone going into my apartment stealing my belongings, he was shocked when I told him who it was. He left after about three hours, this was also the last visit that the two of us would ever have with one another.

Janet, Louis's sister in-law, had also been talking to me recently about her husband, she said, that after four years, he would be getting out of prison in two weeks, and that she would like to know if I would marry the two of them, she had been a very faithful member in the church while Michael was in prison, and she said that she wanted to do what she knew was the right thing. I was a little confused, you see, I had already married the two of them once, so I needed some clarification, well she said, their early years had been very turbulent, and unknown to most people, the two of them had been divorced for nearly fifteen years.

Janet said that as a young woman, twenty-one years old, with four children, she had gone to apply for some government assistance, and when they questioned her about her marital status, she had lied and told the case worker that she did not know where her husband was, they were accustomed to this, so they told her that if she wanted any assistance at all, she would have to allow them to set up an appointment with their legal-aid department, and start divorce proceedings, and that then, and only then would they would give her the needed assistance, and that they would handle the rest of it from there, she consented, and they were legally divorced not long after this.

Upon Michael's release, she called me wanting to know if the two of them could come over to my apartment, I told her that she needed to call Louis, and that he would handle everything. Louis told the two of them to come over to his house, and that he would bring them up to see me, so upon arriving at Louis's house, he called me and told me that they were on their way up to my apartment.

They wanted to keep everything private, seeing as though most people thought that they were still married, Louis brought the two of them up, and I married them right there in my living room, and the three of them left.

As I sat there in my apartment after the three of them left, I pondered the rich history that I had had with the entire Timms family, just among those siblings alone, I had performed twelve wedding ceremonies, some of them, their first and second, but never a funeral.

Bishop bright, the chief disciple of our great organization, yes, the very same one that had been in that supposed two year position since the founder had died about fifteen years ago, had from someone gotten the word, that I wasn't in the best of health, so he was flying up to see me, he brought along one of his daughters, and his assistant with whom he normally traveled. They called me from the airport about an hour before they arrived. I immediately called Louis and told him I wanted him to be at my apartment by the time they arrived, and he came up right away.

When they arrived, they saw that Louis was there, the two of us were sitting in the living room talking, and the chief's daughter asked if we could talk in private, what they really meant was, could you ask Louis to leave, I told them that anything they wanted, or needed to talk to me about, they were free to speak in front of Louis, he's the one that handles all of my business I told them, and chances are, anything that we would talk about, he'll hear about it from me anyway.

You see what I had learned in my many years in the ministry, is that church-folk don't always tell the truth, now if I had put Louis over my business affairs, and made this man my sole beneficiary, and he knows all of the intricate details of my business affairs, and God has already shown me, that my days were numbered, what secret could I possibly have from Louis, unknown to them, it was I, who had told him I wanted him there anyway, now why would I ask him to leave now, oh I knew what they wanted. I've been in this way for a very long time, and if they could have talked to me in private, well the three of them could have said that I said something, that I really didn't say, and might have even persuaded Louis that I had said it, unless he were there, to hear for himself exactly what went on, that's why I told them, Louis stays.

They all wanted to pretend that they were so concerned with me and my welfare, to see if all was well, or if I needed anything from them. I told them that I was just getting by, and that the medicine gets quite expensive, and that I had even called down to headquarters a few times, to see if they would send me a little something out of our benevolence fund, the one that had been established just for the elderly pastors that might have a financial need. The chief did say that he had gotten my messages, he apologized, and had his daughter write me a check right there on the spot.

Now the daughter took her turn to talk, and their true motives were now revealed, Bishop she said, talking to me, what about your business affairs, what about them I said, well she said, are they in order, or would you like me to draw up some paperwork, just in case you wanted to leave any special instructions should anything ever happen to you, Louis has everything under control, and he knows exactly what he needs to do, should anything ever happen to me.

I thanked them all for coming, and told them that I needed my rest, I told them that Louis would show them out. After escorting them to the door, Louis came back and sat down, I showed him the check they had written to me, and I laughed, I told him, that I honestly thought that this was a slap in the face, they wrote me a check for one-hundred dollars, most of my prescriptions cost more than that I said, I told Louis that I had just about had my fill of church-folk, because

"CHURCH-FOLK SOME MESSED-UP FOLK"

Bishop Bright and I had come up together, but time had changed him, he had also let his family influence him in some underhanded dealings related to the church, he brought this particular daughter with him, thinking that she had something on me from my early years in the church that might alter or cloud my thinking.

Job 38:3

"Gird up now thy loins like a man: for I will demand of thee, and answer thou me."

I instructed Louis what he was to do upon my death, and the only person that I specifically told him that I wanted him to give anything to upon my death, was my secretary, Gladys Gunn, and what I told him that I was bequeathing to her, was my wheelchair, I might explain the reason for this later.

1st Corinthians 13:11

"When I was a child, I spake as a child, I understood as a child, I thought as a child: but when I became a man, I put away childish things."

I told Louis that it was now time to stand up and be a man, that because from henceforth, he would have a great responsibility ahead of him, and that he would meet up with great opposition from many that he did not expect it from. I also told Louis that it was time out for foolishness, and that just as Paul had told Timothy in the first letter that he had written to him, it reads as thus:

1st Timothy 4:12

"Let no man despise thy youth; but be thou an example of the believers, in word, in conversation, in charity, in spirit, in faith, in purity."

Its two weeks before Thanksgiving, and according to:

Psalms 90:10

"The days of our years are threescore years and ten; and if by reason of strength they be fourscore years, yet is there strength labour and sorrow; for it is soon cut off, and we fly away."

God doesn't owe me anything, he has brought me from 1905 to 1988, that's longer than he promised, I feel that I am now living on borrowed time, like the longer that I live, I'm shortening someone else's life.

My nephew Perry came to town to visit me today, I had not seen him in fifteen years. I only had one brother, and he had died thirty one years ago, this was his only son, we sat there and reminisced over the olden days. I told him how very glad I was, that he had thought enough of me, to come by and see me. You see once I had gotten into the church, I had become estranged from the biggest portion of my family members.

Louis stopped by, on his way from work today, as was his custom, I introduced the two of them, and he sat there a while with us, and the three of us talked for nearly another two hours. One of the things that I rarely talked about, was my personal life before I came to pastor here, and that was to anyone, including Louis, but now one of the things that I asked Perry to do for me, was to see if he could locate my two sons, and tell them I would like to see them, you see I had two biological sons, whom I had not seen, since before moving here in 1964, and Perry said that he would be sure and get the message to them.

As Perry was preparing to leave, Louis told him that he would go out with him, and they left together around 8:30 that evening.

James 4:14

"Whereas ye know not what shall be on the morrow. For what is your life? It is even a vapour, that appeareth for a little time, and then vanisheth away."

Just to ponder our human frailty, can be overwhelming at time, I often told Louis that as a young man I had heard the proverb, that you are once a man, and twice a child, the revelation of this is now quite clear, for as a child, I had relied on someone to take care of my every need, I have now reverted back to this state.

1st Peter 1:24

"For all flesh is as grass, and all the glory of man as the flower of grass, the grass withereth, and the flower thereof falleth away."

Louis has now hired me two nurses, that come in to take care of me seven days a week, just doing my everyday chores now, is quite exhausting, but I know, that I must go the way that all flesh goes. On Sunday mornings, Louis himself now has to come upstairs, just to help me get dressed and roll me down to the car, and in the evening, he has to roll me back up, and help me get undressed before he can go to his own home.

The last Sunday in the year, just happened to fall on Christmas day, as usual, we went to church, I just had a strange feeling to come over me this day though. Louis took me up in the pulpit, he, along with everyone else, could see how unstable I was, Louis stood by me in the pulpit that Sunday morning, the whole time that I preached. When church was over I had a very eerie feeling, and as it was time to leave, I began to cry uncontrollably, I wanted to shake hands and speak to all of the members, and to tell them how good it was to see them, and to say to them one last good-bye, I loved them, even thou I knew that

"CHURCH-FOLK SOME MESSED-UP FOLK"

These are all of the people that I have nurtured, loved, prayed for and with, visited in the jails and hospitals, performed many of their, or their families wedding ceremonies, christened them, as well as some of their children, I have eulogized many of their friends and loved ones. But this night, God himself had revealed to me, that this was the last I would ever see most of them, or that I would ever be at the church alive again.

The memories that I had there weren't all good ones, but we were a family, and as with any family, we must weather the storms of life together, the good, the bad and the ugly. There are often times that we will sustain many wounds from one another, and may be subjected to great heartache, and love may dissipate, but they will always maintain a place in your heart of hearts.

Proverbs 18:24

"A man that hath friends must shew himself friendly: and there is a friend that sticketh closer than a brother."

That following Monday, I had a doctors appointment, I went to the hospital and was not at all surprised when they admitted me, Louis came to see me after he had gotten off work that evening, one of the nurses walked by and commented, I see your son is here to see, I said to her, he has always stuck by me, through thick and thin, Louis was my closest friend.

In the hospital, and at my apartment, I had Louis listed as my son, and most of the people that saw him, would often comment on how nice my son was, and all that I could ever say, was oh yes he is. I do not believe, nor have I ever believed, that Death catches the child of God by surprise, when I left my apartment that morning, I had a gut feeling that I was going to be admitted, so I had already given Louis that coveted briefcase the night before, when he had taken me home.

Matthew 7:22-23

"Many will say to me in that day, Lord, Lord, have we not prophesied in thy name? and in thy name have cast out devils? And in thy name done many wonderful works? And then will I profess unto them, I never knew you: depart from me, ye that work iniquity."

Now that Louis is here with me, we began to talk, many things will happen in a man's life, I told him, and many people will try and fool you, but whatever you do, don't leave God, never let go of his hand, and many people you will see, will dip in and out of the church, at their convenience, but don't you play the hokey pokey with God. I also told him that he should not believe everything that people tell him, many will tell you that they are in spiritual warfare, whereas in reality, they are simply dancing with the enemy, and of utmost importance, never, ever, mistake religion, for relationship, many will tell you that they know God, and that they have a relationship with him, when what they really mean is they know of him, or about him, Paul also told Timothy about this in;

2nd Timothy 3:5

"Having a form of godliness, but denying the power thereof: from such turn away."

I told Louis, that there are certain individuals that you should not even want to keep company with. Everyone that presents himself as a friend, does not have your best interest at hand, many that will smile in your face, would cut you down like grass given the opportunity.

Genesis 4:1

"And Adam knew Eve his wife; and she conceived and bare Cain, and said, I have gotten a man from the Lord"

Likewise, this is how we should want to know our God, we must have an intimate relationship with him, Eve didn't conceive by knowing of Adam, or about Adam, but she had an intimate relationship with him.

Philippians 1:6

"Being confident of this very thing, that he which hath begun a good work in you will perform it until the day of Jesus Christ."

I talked to Louis long and hard that evening, I wanted to be able to rest in peace, knowing that the work God had began in him, was not a total waste of God's time and talent, Louis was there until almost 10:00 P.M. that night, neither of us knew, that this would be the last conversation that the two would ever have on this side of heaven. The point that I'm trying to make is, that God will keep you, if you want to be kept.

Once Louis left it was my turn to talk to God, you see I haven't always been saved, and even when I was, I too, have also had my share of short-comings and indiscretions, but I have always had a heart for God, and for the things of God, I again repented of all of the things that I had done wrong in my life, that I knew God was not well pleased with, I had tried to do the best that I could, with the hand that I was dealt in life, I had tried to make it up to people, but most of all, I had tried to make it up to God.

As individuals, and as Christians, we have gotten caught up in a vicious seasonal cycle, we're obedient to God's word, then we get caught in some sin, God then has to give us some harsh correction or judgment, we then repent, we then become obedient to God's word again, where then this cycle starts all over again.

As the bible says in

Jude 3,

"We must earnestly contend for the faith which was once delivered unto the saints."

If the only capacity that we want to serve God in, is as advisers, then we are not serving him at all. Remember years ago that there was a very popular bumper sticker that read

"GOD IS MY CO-PILOT"

If God is your co-pilot, you had better switch seats, the only spiritual entity willing to go along with us for the ride, is Satan. Ready or not, all of this that we call life, will someday come to an end, and all of the things that we have valued and cherished, will someday be left behind for someone else to enjoy, whatever we may possess, houses, cars, money, positions, intellect, ambitions, plans, to-do lists, and all that seemed at one time so important to us, will now fade away.

That night as I dozed off to sleep, I felt a sense of peace and calm, come over me, and in the spirit, the Lord took me on a journey. The next morning when the nurse came in to give me my medication, she could not awaken me, I had lapsed into a coma. The doctors came in and ran all the routine tests that they normally run, but my fate was now sealed.

I laid there for the next thirty days, in a coma. Louis came by to see me everyday. God was purging me, Louis would come in the room, he would see me lying there in a coma, with tears rolling down my face, Louis knew what God was doing to me, and so did I. He still came by faithfully, every-day, with the hope that one day there would be a turn for the better. There never was, I had reached the end of my journey called life.

5

"THE END OF AN ERA"

Deuteronomy 31:14

"And the LORD said unto Moses, Behold, thy days approach that thou must die."

Psalms 116:15

*"Precious in the sight of the LORD is the **death of his** saints."*

2 Corinthians 5:8

"We are confident, I say, and willing rather to be absent from the body, and to be present with the Lord."

Philippians 1:21

"For to me to live is Christ, and to die is gain."

We cannot possibly expect to live always, there are successors out there to replace each and every one of us, yet when this life is ending, we simply do not want to let go of it, simply out of fear of the unknown. If we really understood how beautiful, life after death was, it would take away from death, some of its mystery, but we don't know, therefore fear takes hold of us, and the closer we get to death, the more fearful many of us become. If we have faith in God, we should not fear death, if we fear death, we need to take spiritual inventory of our lives and how we have lived them.

It was during this somber period, lying there in my hospital bed, that the Lord of my salvation showed me the great and marvelous things to come, to the point that I did not want to hold on to this life any longer. I had studied and taught the word of God for over fifty years, and even in my wildest and most vivid imaginations, I could not comprehend, what God has in store for those that love him and keep his commandments,

1 Corinthians 2:9

"But as it is written, Eye hath not seen, nor ear heard, neither have entered into the heart of man, the things which God hath prepared for them that love him."

My heartfelt prayer, was one not so much of a selfish desire, but one of love and concern, mainly for Louis, but also for that entire Timms family, who all, had held a very special place in my heart for a very long time.

Now let us take a little walk through the bible, many have taught, and many are taught, that at the point of death, your consciousness ceases to exist, that concept is based mostly on this one passage from the bible:

Ecclesiastes 9:5

*"For **the living know** that they shall die: but the dead know not any thing, neither have they any more a reward; for the memory of them is forgotten."*

We must try to put all things in there proper perspective, this is an Old Testament passage, where when men died during that dispensation of time, they were under the law, men died only having this hope, that a saviour would one day would come. But we are no longer under the law, we are living in the dispensation of Jesus Christ, where men are under the grace and truth of Jesus Christ himself, who came to provide a better way for you and I, than had been provided for those who had already died, and that were under the law.

Hebrews 11:39-40

"And these all, having obtained a good report through faith, received not the promise: God having provided some better thing for us, that they without us should not be made perfect."

The hope of all who died before Jesus Christ came in the flesh, died with the hope, that one day the promised Savior would come, and deliver their souls from an eternal torment.

1 Peter 3:19-20

"By which also he went and **preached unto th***e spirits in prison; Which sometime were disobedient, when once the longsuffering of God waited in the days of Noah, while the ark was a preparing, wherein few, that is, eight souls were saved by water."*

Those who had their hope in a future Messiah, had their just souls delivered by Jesus Christ, when he went into hell and preached to them for those three days, letting them all know that their deliverer had come.

Revelation 6:9-10

"And when he had opened the fifth seal, I saw under the altar the souls of them that were slain for the word of God, and for the testimony which they held: And they cried with a loud voice, saying, How long, O Lord, holy and true, dost thou not judge and avenge our blood on them that dwell on the earth?"

Now we find the New Testament saints, who upon their deaths, are in a fully conscious state.

2 Kings 20:1-6

"In those days was Hezekiah sick unto death. And the prophet Isaiah the son of Amoz came to him, and said unto him, Thus saith the LORD, Set thine house in order; for thou shalt die, and not live. Then he turned his face to the wall, and prayed unto the LORD, saying, I beseech thee, O LORD, remember now how I have walked before thee in truth and with a perfect heart, and have done that which is good in thy sight. And Hezekiah wept sore. And it came to pass, afore Isaiah was gone out into the middle court, that the word of the LORD came to him, saying, Turn again, and tell Hezekiah the captain of my people, Thus saith the LORD, the God of David thy father, I have heard thy prayer, I have seen thy tears: behold, I will heal thee: on the third day thou shalt go up unto the house of the LORD. And I will add unto thy days fifteen years; and I will deliver thee and this city out of the hand of the king of Assyria; and I will defend this city for mine own sake, and for my servant David's sake."

This was my prayer also while laying there, somewhere between life and death, only God knew how I had conducted myself during my lifetime, only God knew the condition of my heart, and that if it would please the Lord, my hearts desire, would be that I be allowed to influence and play some integral part in Louis's life over the next fifteen years. The Lord granted me my wish, and for that reason, Louis couldn't write the book before now anyway, for that reason also, this book will now chronicle the next fifteen years of his life.

I don't want anyone to get the wrong impression, or to think in some manner, that you can converse with the dead in some way, the influence that I wanted to have, was that he would always feel my presence in his heart and in his mind, and to consider them in his actions.

So on my thirty-first day in the hospital, January 26th, 1989, at 10:30 A.M., I breathed my last breath, I gave up the ghost.

Louis was at work when he received the telephone call that morning. He immediately left work, and went directly to the hospital, one of the nurses brought him into the room to where I was still lying, he touched me on the hand, and he thanked the Lord for having had me in his life. He collected my personal belongings, and he left.

On his way home, the Holy Spirit dealt with him, and gave him instructions, he was to immediately go to that large popular funeral home, that handled so many of the funerals in the city there. Louis turned his car around, and did just that, he went in, met with the funeral director, picked out the coffin, and signed the form, making him fully liable for the full payment, then he left and headed for home.

Once he arrived home, he called his parents, and a few other individuals, who would then spread the word. Already I was very pleased with the way he was handling things.

He now had a very busy week ahead of him. He notified the rental office at my apartment, he called and set up an appointment with my attorney to execute my last will and testament, he put the program and the order of service together for the funeral.

Two days later, people began arriving from all over for my funeral. A Bishop's funeral, is filled with pomp and circumstance, and Louis now understood why the Holy Spirit had directed him, to go directly from the hospital, to the funeral home and make arrangements. All the other Bishops wanted to talk to him, and tell him how they thought things should be carried out, the mentality that Louis was operating under and made known to each of them, was that whoever wants to help him pay for this funeral, could talk about how they wanted the order of services carried out, not one person gave Louis a penny, or was willing to, therefore they all became very quiet, you know why, because

"CHURCH-FOLK SOME MESSED-UP FOLK"

The day of my funeral arrived, and my niece flew into town along with my two sons, and my twenty-two year old granddaughter, whom I had never even seen before, and the way this young woman carried on during the services, you would have almost thought that we had lived in the house together. Although Louis had outlined the order of services, and he had told all that were involved, that he would be the one reading the obituary, would you believe that they still had their own agendas. Louis had sent the obituaries out to the printer two days earlier, and they were supposed to be back at the church by now, but no one seemed to know where they were.

Exactly fifteen minutes before the start of the funeral, Louis was given an obituary, and right there printed in black and white, it read, "Reading of the obituary" Gladys Gunn. Now remember Gladys, this was my secretary, Louis was livid, he thought to himself, now if this is printed here, someone changed this two days ago, when he had first sent them out to the printer, Louis stormed upstairs, flung open the door to what had been my office, where Gladys and five of the Bishops were sitting in a meeting, he looked at Gladys, and he asked her who was the one designated to read the obituary, well said Gladys nonchalantly, all of the Bishops wanted me to read it, Louis looked her straight in the face and said, I would suggest to you, that by the time the Master of Ceremony gets to that part on the program, that you all have this straightened out, and he walked out, and for those of you that may wonder, Louis was the one that read it.

As expected, all of the other Bishops, stood up at the appropriate time, to have words, and what words they did have, they all said such wonderful things about me, knowing that for the most part, many of them had never really cared that much for me. I had always been a little too outspoken for most of them, and I wasn't willing to go along with a lot of the things that they had proposed, and at the sight of the almighty dollar, most of them were a little too easily compromised. Money today, has too much of a stronghold on us, even in our churches today, where it really should not have, and for a few measly coins, many of us have compromised our ways right into hell.

As I had grown older, me and money, had sort of fallen out, the one thing that I really wanted, it couldn't buy me, that was my health back. I was not as willing to compromise as some of the other, younger Bishops were, and I do understand their plight, but now, I must be true, first to my God, and then to myself.

Being in the ministry, has changed tremendously in the last fifty years, it is no longer a calling, being a minister has now become an occupation, anyone out of work, or not wanting to work, anyone getting out of prison, anyone going into prison, all of a sudden have been called into the ministry. If you say that you have been called into the ministry, and it is not accompanied, by a change in your lifestyle, you are a liar, and the truth is not in you. He that preaches the gospel, must first live by it himself, but greed has crept in, and this will be the downfall to a great many people, who might otherwise have done a great work, in the furtherance of the gospel.

After the funeral, Louis got into the funeral home limousine, to go to the cemetery, and my niece and my two sons unexpectedly got in there with him, they all introduced themselves to one another, and Louis told the eldest one that he appeared to be about my size, that he might be interested in some of my clothes, his response was, I'm more interested in knowing where his money is, to Louis surprise. Louis also told them that my nephew Perry, their first cousin, had been there a couple of months earlier to see me, and that I had told him to get them word that I would like to see them, they told Louis that they had gotten the message, and that they had always known where I was, and they if they had wanted to see me, they would have done so. Again they asked Louis, where is his money, Louis gave them my attorneys number, and told them that he could answer any questions that they might have.

Upon leaving the cemetery, and returning to the church to eat, the atmosphere had changed tremendously. The chief disciple was a very busy man, and he was scheduled to fly back home that night, therefore he called a meeting right after everyone had eaten. Louis was called into the meeting, and questioned about certain business matters pertaining to my affairs, he was very well prepared, he pulled a copy of my will from his pocket, handed it to Gladys, and told her to read it in its entirety, to all who were present.

They were all noticeably disturbed, at what they heard of course, and the chief disciple said to Louis, well, all I know is that your Bishop promised me his limousine, Louis smiled at him and said, I'm sorry, but that's my car, and the title is in my name, well what does the church get he asked, nothing that I know of, Louis very politely replied.

I had been the Diocese Bishop over the state that I resided in, upon my passing, that position went to the only other Bishop in our state, Bishop Green. The one thing that I had not yet covered was who it was that had gone into my apartment and stolen from me, well it was my sweet secretary Gladys Gunn and Bishop Green, and most of the members knew this.

That very same night, the chief disciple, and the new state Diocese Bishop, appointed my successor, right then and there, they were bringing in a young man that had a long history with this great organization, however he was not yet a seasoned preacher.

I had often told the members, that when I was dead and gone, the generosity that they had all grown so accustomed to, would die with me, and that a new, and younger pastor, with a family of his own to care for would come in, with different needs, and he would make some of those very same ones, who had been hoping that I would die, long for the day that they had me as their pastor.

In many organizations, the assistant would step into the role of pastor, but nepotism was alive and well, and when they appointed Elder Jonah Logan, as my successor, it became quite clear to some in the church, who was behind this, not only did they appoint him that night, but they said that it would be three months before he could relocate, and that the members there were to save all of the money for him until he arrived, and that my assistant, Reverend Al Timms, would take over until he Elder Logan had moved here.

So just to make sure you have it all correct, lets go over once again, Elder Logan will be moving here within the next three months, during that three month period, you are to save all of the monies coming into the church, for him, he will also be collecting the monies at his own church, until he leaves there in three months, and Reverend Timms, is to carry on for those three months until Elder Logan arrives, with no compensation, I hope you've got all this, now aren't

"CHURCH-FOLK SOME MESSED-UP FOLK"

That week of my funeral, after Louis called my attorney to have my "Last Will and Testament" probated, various members of the church began questioning Louis about all of my worldly possessions, asking him what did he think he would be doing with the contents from my apartment, and he told them that he had not decided on anything for certain, and that if someone wanted something of mine, to let him know, and he would do what he could to accommodate most of them.

For Louis, the task at hand, was to now clean out the contents of my apartment. There were certain things that I could have, and probably should have discarded, but I chose not to, because I just really didn't care anymore, if he, or someone else were to come across them.

All of my suits were tailor made, and due to the fact that my sons had declined the offer, even to look at them, Louis gave the majority of them to Goodwill Industries.

Louis did also receive a call from an attorney, that my biological sons had retained, this attorney told Louis, that the two of them would be willing to settle for ten-thousand dollars apiece, Louis thought for a moment about part of the contents of my will, particularly the part that read "For my own personal reasons, I do not want either of my sons to have anything", and Louis told their attorney, that he would have to contact my attorney, that was the last time that Louis ever heard anything from, of or even about my sons.

To you people that think someone owes you something just because you're related to them, let me dispel this rumor, because there's just no truth to it. Many times, people wonder why an individual would leave his estate in such a mess for his spouse, children or other relatives to deal with, well most of the time it's quite deliberate. The life that many people have lived, or the way that they treat, or have treated someone, has a tremendous effect on an individuals heart, and to many, this plays a very important part when it comes time to plan out ones estate.

Until Louis and I formed the strong bond that we had, I had not even written my Last Will and Testament, simply because, I really didn't care where any of my worldly possessions ended up, once I died, in one sense it had at one time sort of amused me, thinking that when I die, everyone would question how I could leave things in such a mess, I would often think to myself, let them fight over it and sort out the mess. The way that I had reasoned it all out was, that for those who thought that they had something coming from me, although they had not been there for me, if they get anything, they would have to go through some trouble for it, and I often felt that if everything I had went to the state, that would be just fine with me also, I just didn't care anymore.

Someone might ask, why not leave it to the church, this, at one time had been my original intention, but because I have seen so many mean, evil, low-down and narrow minded individuals in the church, and I'm not talking about all lay people either, some so called church-folk are much worse off than those that claim to have no relationship with God at all, therefore I had also ruled the church out, my feeling was that if you were going to perpetrate, it certainly wasn't going to be with any of my money, and I was thoroughly convinced that the way that I had paid my way through life, I didn't owe anybody anything.

Louis told Carol, that this summer they were going to have their best vacation ever, he told her that he had decided that the family was going to go to Disneyworld, he set the wheels in motion, and made the appropriate reservations. Unknown to most people, my death, certain individuals actions, as well as all the other circumstances surrounding my funeral, had really taken its toll on Louis, it had shaken his faith tremendously and had left him in sort of a state of uncertainty, but God had him in the hallow of his hand.

6

"A TALE OF TWO DEATHS"

Romans 6:23

"For the wages of sin is death; but the gift of God is eternal life through Jesus Christ our Lord."

Romans 8:6

"For to be carnally minded is death; but to be spiritually minded is life and peace."

2 Corinthians 4:12

"So then death worketh in us, but life in you."

We serve a God, who sits high and looks low, we cannot and should not expect to do any and everything that we want to do, and then continue to expect the blessings of a holy and righteous God to be over our lives. For us to be spiritually dead, this will eventually lead us to an eternal death and permanent separation from the almighty God, therefore, at all cost, we must guard our hearts from all that would do us harm.

As I had also promised before, that we would get back to Rod, Louis's cousin, not his brother yet, I haven't forgotten about him either, but let me regress, about six years before my death, at the tender age of 21, Rod's parents had been killed, Rod was left with an apartment building, a couple of automobiles, a nice little savings account and a very troubled life. Rod was his parents only child, therefore he was their sole beneficiary, and due to the fact that he and Louis were so close in age, the two of them had become extremely close, and had remained this way, for the entire period leading right up to my death.

Rod had gone through some very tumultuous times in his short life-time, and he had always confided in Louis, even telling him that the first year after the death of his parents, that he had gone through with every penny that they had left for him, as well as taking out a first and second mortgage on the apartment building.

Now two years after the death of Rod's parents, and four years before my own death, Louis had shared with me that Rod had become extremely depressed, and that he had planned on killing his then girlfriend and him-self, luckily the day that he had actually planned all of this, he called Louis and told him he needed someone to talk to, and he asked Louis if he would come over to his apartment, where there, he shared with Louis, that he had gone through so much in his lifetime, and that lately he had been feeling depressed the majority of the time, and that he was just tired of it all.

What he told Louis was, that now, in addition to the inner turmoil that he was struggling with, he had just found out that his girlfriend Amber, had been unfaithful to him, which was now more than he could handle. Rod told Louis that the main reason he had called him over was just to talk to him, to tell him how much he loved and appreciated him, to thank him for always being there for him whenever he would call, for never judging him, and that this was the last time that he would ever see him again because this very evening he was going to kill not only himself, but his girlfriend Amber also.

Once Louis left Rod's apartment that afternoon, he could not stop thinking about Rod, and their earlier conversation, fortunately for Amber, remember that was Rod's girlfriend, Louis knew what time she normally arrived home from work. So that evening, Louis went back over to Rod's apartment, he didn't see his car, so he decided to just sit there in front of the apartment for a little while and wait. It wasn't long before Louis saw the bus pull up and Amber stepped down out of it, she crossed the street and began walking towards the apartment building, Louis then exited his vehicle and began walking towards her, she smiled when she saw Louis, she spoke to him, and not seeing Rod's car, naturally she was curious as to why he was there, Louis told her that he just wanted to walk her inside the apartment to make sure that everything was alright, again she smiled and without giving it any further thought said alright.

Now ladies, think about this, how many of you would have just said okay to this, and you men, what would you have said if your woman or wife, had agreed to this so nicely, and had then been assaulted in some form or even raped, we would have said that she should have known better, but God, when God is in the plan, he goes ahead of us, and he prepares the situation at hand, so that all will be smooth sailing.

In this particular situation, the wrong attitude could and very well would, have cost many women their very lives, those that may have looked at him and scoffed, I don't need you to walk me into my apartment, she could have simply refused, saying no that's okay, I don't want Rod to come home and catch you leaving or something, and get the wrong idea, all of these things that she could have said, with justification, that made lots of sense, but she simply said okay.

As Louis and Amber entered the apartment building, Louis walked first, into the bedroom, then he came out and walked into the bathroom, then into the kitchen, he looked at Amber, who then asked, why did you think something would be wrong? She had no idea, relating to the events that had transpired earlier that day, or even that Louis and Rod had talked at all, or what the gist of their conversation had been, not wanting to alarm her, Louis said, I was just worried that something might be wrong, then he said to her, just tell Rod that I stopped by, and he told Amber that he would see her later.

He then turned and headed for the door, just before he reached it, Rod jumped out from a small hall closet near the front door, holding a large caliber pistol in his hand, as he looked at Louis, he said to him, I thought I heard your voice, why did you have to come back?, to which Louis explained, I came back because I didn't want to see you hurt yourself, or anyone else for that matter, Amber stood quietly in the background, she was visibly shaken over all of this. Upon staying and conversing with Rod for awhile, Rod came to grips with himself, ending that standoff peacefully.

Amber on the other hand, was a very intelligent young lady, and from this point on, she realized that she needed to distance herself from Rod, but even to do this in the wrong way could still put her very life in jeopardy, it took her nearly four months, but she finally did it, she rid herself of Rod, and the cleverest thing she did, was to make Rod think that it was all his idea to break it off, many of you ladies out there know exactly what I'm talking about.

So what does Rod and all this have to do with church-folk anyway you might ask, now remember Rod had already been taken into a back room at some church, and had been taught how to speak in tongues, now keep this in mind, that anything that doesn't come from God himself, is a counterfeit, there are only two spirits in operation, and we all know what they are, and everyone operates under the influence of one of these spirits, so let us be real, that's all I'm saying, the spirit of the true and living God, is the only thing that can and will stand the test of time.

Please follow along with me, I'm trying to make a point, and will get back to our rightful place in this story, and I can assure you that it will all tie together in the end.

Rod had already began seeing someone else, which made the transition from being with Amber that much easier, especially for her, he had slowly

began drifting away from Amber, towards a new, and much younger con-
quest, this girls name was Rita, she was only sixteen years old at the time,
and very pure to Rod, who had been with quite a few women in his short
lifetime, and had tried just about any and everything that a young man his
age could possibly want to try.

Rita had had a troubled life, she had been brought up in foster homes
for the most part, which made her cater to Rod all the more, therefore anything that he would ask her to do, she did without any questions, she even
tolerated the occasional beatings that he subjected her to. The one thing
that I would like to point out though, is that even iron will eventually wear
out. This to date, was the longest relationship that Louis had ever seen
Rod have with a woman.

Two years before the death of his parents, Rod had a girlfriend, who
had also bore him a son, after which, the two of them had broken things
off, but the year after his parents death, Rod began to harass her, trying to
control and keep tabs on her, she was afraid of him and moved in with relatives, over a thousand miles away just to get away from him. Louis now
thought that for the most part, everything was going pretty well with Rod
and Rita, many times he'd arrive home to find the two of them sitting in
his driveway waiting for him, not only was Louis his best friend, he was
family, and this made Rod draw all the closer to him.

Rita, being as young as she was, had never even had a job, therefore she
looked to Rod for everything, and he took very good care of her, as far as
the basic necessities of life go, you see he rarely worked himself, but due to
the fact that he was the one that owned the apartment building, he didn't
have to pay any rent, and the income from the other units took care of
them fairly well. Not really one for wanting to work much, he tried very
hard to keep his expenses low.

In late 1987, Rita became pregnant, Rod was ecstatic, this he felt would
be bone of his bone and flesh of his flesh, someone he could love uncondi-
tionally, and someone that he felt could reciprocate those feelings.

That following year, the summer of 1988, Rita gave birth to a beautiful
baby girl, and this child truly did make Rod want to stand up and be a
responsible man, she melted Rod's heart, the name that they chose for her

was Annie. That year he also became a changed man, he rose to the occasion and took on his paternal responsibility, he went out and got a job, and for the first time in his life, he even began talking about marriage. Those first few months were absolutely wonderful, however, Rita was still a very young girl, and she was now beginning to come into herself. Most weekends now, Rita had began to go out and party, with a sister she had found, they had both been brought up in different foster care homes and had had little contact over the years, but now that they were grown and had located each other, they had sort of formed a bond with one another. It wasn't long before she began hanging out at an Aunts house, sometimes spending the entire weekend there.

One day while at work, Rod overheard two young men talking, one of the young men was telling the other about his new girlfriend, he went on to tell him that she was living with an aunt, that she had a baby girl less than a year old named Annie, and that she had not too long ago, broken up with the child's father. Rod maintained his composure in front of the young men, never saying a word, but he was livid. He went home that evening, and he beat Rita unmercifully, she told Rod that this was the last beating that she would ever take, from him, or anyone else for that matter.

The following morning while Rod was at work, Rita gathered up some things for her and Annie, and the two of them left the apartment. When Rod came home from work and found them gone, he became worried, he called her aunt searching for her, but she wasn't there, however later that evening, the aunt had gotten word to her, and Rita called Rod back. She told him that she would never be returning to that apartment, and as far as she was concerned, their relationship was over. Rod told her that he wanted to see his daughter, she told him that she would never keep his daughter from him, and that anytime he wanted to see her, that she would drop the child off at her aunts and that he could pick her up there.

Rod did just that, he would call the aunt, who would have the child at her house anytime he wanted to see her, and this went on for almost two months. Finally one day Rod called Louis, he asked him to go somewhere with him, they went to the shopping mall, where Rod told Louis that they had never had a picture taken together, they stopped in a kiosk, there in the middle of the mall, and the two of them had their only picture taken together, from there, Rod told Louis that he had already made an appointment with his attorney there in the mall, and would appreciate it if Louis would accompany him there, which he did.

Upon arriving at the attorneys, Rod had him draw up his "Last Will and Testament", and he named Louis as his executor and sole beneficiary, he also had the attorney put in there, that if anything should ever happen to him, that he wanted his cousin, Louis Timms, to raise his daughter Annie, as his very own, this whole ordeal came as quite a surprise to Louis.

Upon leaving the mall, Rod explained everything to Louis in the car. He told Louis about the problems he had been having with Rita, he told him about the conversation he had overheard the two young men having on his job, he also told him that he had been looking for Rita for two weeks, to kill her, but the twist there was, he wanted to catch her with the young man in question that he worked with, because his intents were to kill the two of them, as well as himself.

Rod reminded Louis that a few years earlier, he had talked him out of doing this to he and Amber, but this time he said, Louis, I'll listen to anything that you have to say, but this time you're not going to talk me out of it. Louis made sure that he talked to Rod everyday from this point on, just trying to give him some words of encouragement, hoping that if he could just get Rod to see, that these things happen in life, and if we could just get pass them, brighter days were ahead. He pleaded with Rod, to pray about this matter.

This now brings us back to our present place in the story, where Louis had told Carol and the boys, that they were going to go to Disneyworld. Now as the time approached for their appointed vacation, Louis had some last minute details that he felt he needed to wrap up.

Since my death, earlier that year, there had been so many tension filled episodes in the church. For months, Louis had been drawn to a little church around the corner from his house, there was a sign out front that read, "Bible-based and Bible-Believing", which was all that Louis had ever been searching for.

Elder Logan had now relocated there, and had been the pastor there for the last four months. The latter part of July, after morning service, Louis went into his office to talk to him, he told him that so much had gone on in his life, that he felt like he needed a break, he told him that the next Sunday he would be on vacation, and the Sunday following that, he would be visiting a small church around the corner from his home, so for the next two Sundays he and his family would not be there.

Louis had planned on leaving for vacation, the first Tuesday in August, he knew that the first Monday was the ending of the six month waiting period, and he needed that day to close out my estate. He had reserved a car, and was to pick it up early that Tuesday morning, and he Carol and the boys would drive down to Florida.

It doesn't really matter what you see on the exterior, Louis had his own set of problems to deal with and he was not that pleased with his own life right about now, he had shared with only one individual, that the spirit of the Lord had clearly revealed to him that he shouldn't take that drive to Florida, but he had become so despondent, that he had already said to himself, that even if he did not make it back home alive, he really didn't care, and that he was going anyway, and regardless of the outcome, nothing was going to stop him, now mind you, that's what Louis said.

Again, but God, this is what most of us forget to factor in, in our lives, we may all have our own agendas, but if and when God chooses to override them, God will show his sovereignty, and when we choose to say that we are going to do something and nothing will stop us, we need to say nothing will stop us but God.

Isaiah 46:10

"God knows the end from the beginning, and has declared from the ancient of days, the things that are not yet done."

If God has a task for any of us to do, you will do it one way or the other. God was not giving up on Louis, there was too much at stake, too much he still needed to know, and too much that he still needed to do in Louis's life.

That first Monday in August, was also the first day that Louis had started his vacation, he went into my attorney's office first thing that morning, signed the proper paperwork to close out my estate, went to the bank and wrapped up everything there. He and Carol then went to the store to pick up some last minute items that they needed fir their trip, and finally they headed for home.

Less than five minutes after arriving home, Louis's phone rang, it was two-o'clock in the afternoon, and it was his cousin Rod, calling to tell him that he had been looking for him all morning, and to ask him if it would be okay if he came over. Louis explained to him that they had been out shopping most of the morning, getting their last minute items together for their trip that they were leaving for the following day, and Louis told Rod that it would be fine if he wanted to come over.

Within five minutes, Rod was pulling into the driveway, his birthday had been one month before this, and he was driving the automobile Louis had given him for his birthday, he had Annie with him, she was asleep, he came in and laid her down on the couch, he began to tell Louis that he could not go on like this any longer, he told Louis that the only two people he loved in the whole world, were Louis and his daughter Annie, who was still less than a year old. He then asked Louis if he would go for a ride with him, Louis said that he would, Rod asked Carol if Annie could stay there on the couch asleep, and she said she could.

As they walked out of the house, Rod asked Louis if they could go in Louis's car, Louis said that they could, Rod said, and one other thing, Louis said that I already know, you want to drive and he handed Rod his car keys. As they were riding, Louis said to Rod, you wanted to drive, because only you know the places that you want to go, and you want to go in my car because you're afraid that your car will be recognized, and he asked Rod, why couldn't he just let it go, to which Rod responded, this is the last time that any woman is going to ever do this to me again.

The first house that Rod drove to, he told Louis that this is where the guy that I work, that's been messing around with Rita lives, however he said, I don't see Rita's car, and I was hoping to catch the two of them together, the next house that he drove to, was Rita's aunt, he didn't see her car there either, but he went to the door and knocked anyway, and asked if she was there, someone inside told him that she wasn't, Rod then came back to the car, got inside and they headed back to Louis's house. Rod also told Louis that he was right on the money as to why he wanted to drive his car also, and he told Louis that he understood him better than anyone else ever had.

What Louis understood, that Rod did not, was that in life, there are certain cycles that you are going to go through, and that at any given time, you are either coming out of a storm in your life, you are in the midst of a storm in your life, or you are headed into a storm in your life, best of all Louis understood, that without Jesus Christ in your life, it is much more difficult to weather these storms.

Louis understood Rod, because they were a cut from the same tree, what Rod and many other people don't realize is, that whatever problems you may be having, you may be telling them to an individual, that in many instances, is worse off than you yourself are, and when life seems to be so perplexing to you, the last thing you need, is to turn to someone else for help, and have them dump all their problems on you, one of the things that Louis had learned very early in life, was to take all of his problems to God.

They arrived back at Louis's house, all this had transpired in a span of about forty-five minutes time, and Annie was still asleep. Carol had prepared some food, and asked Rod if would like to eat with them, and he said that he would, so she fixed both their plates, and Rod and Louis sat there and ate spaghetti, meatballs, and coleslaw, a meal that Louis would never forget.

Upon completing their meals, the two of them went back into the living room and continued talking, at approximately three-o'clock that afternoon, Rod made a telephone call to someone, whomever it was that he had called, he heard Rita talking in the background, he abruptly hung the telephone up, grabbed Annie, who was still sleeping, ran out of Louis's house, through Annie into the car, and took off, giving no explanation at all for his actions. Louis didn't think very much of it, because he knew that

Rod was a very troubled man, he simply commented to Carol, I hope that he doesn't go out and do anything foolish.

As Louis was still working out last minute details for his trip, he received a telephone call, it was from one of the large hospitals there in the city, telling him that Rod was there, with a self inflicted gunshot wound to the head, and that he had expired. What they didn't tell him, because they didn't know it at the time, was that Rita was in another hospital across town, with a fatal gunshot wound to the head also.

Louis got into his car, and headed to the hospital, upon arriving, he went to the front desk and explained who he was, and that he had just received a telephone call from them concerning Rod, the attendant explained that the shot had been fatal and that there was nothing that they could do to save him, Louis asked them how it came about that he was the one that they had contacted, they told him that Rod had his name and telephone number written on a piece of paper in his pocket, along with the words "next of kin".

Louis then asked them if he could see Rod, they recommended against it, however Louis told them that Rod had just left his house and that all of this was to unreal to him, they took him to the sixth floor, into a room, where Rod lay, flat on his back, with the tube still in his mouth, Louis touched him and just said one word, why, he then turned to leave and told them that he would get back with them about releasing the body to some-one, they told him that all of that had been taken care of already, he asked by whom, they told him a name, and he said alright, it was the name of a first cousin who Louis knew well and had a good rapport with, therefore he really didn't mind.

Louis left the hospital and went back home, he had a lot of soul search-ing to do, contrary to what anyone else might say or think, Louis knew, that God had sacrificed Rod, so that his life might be spared, still Louis had contemplated driving to Florida, However, upon much reflection, he knew that the trip had been planned for a week long stay, and that the timing now, would not be right, with the demise of Rod and all.

Louis and Carol talked, and they finally decided, that it would probably be the best thing, if they put Florida off. Louis decided that they should go to the amusement park that I had taken them to about two years before my death.

Louis went over to Rod's apartment the next day. Someone had already gone in and removed all of the household furnishings, Louis went upstairs to talk to some of the tenants that he knew there in the building, they told him that another relative of he and Rod's that lived across the street, had been there until about 4:00 A.M. that morning removing items from the apartment.

Louis went over and talked to that relative, who said that he had no idea what they were talking about and that they had to be mistaken, it wasn't him, he told Louis that the only thing that he had were the keys to the apartment, which another relative, who had been at the hospital before Louis arrived had given to him, he did give all of Rod's apartment keys to Louis.

Late that same evening, Louis received a telephone call from Mrs. Booker, Tina's mom, the one who's wedding Byron had been in years before, they were all old friends from church, and occasionally Louis and Mrs. Booker would telephone each other, remember she was Junior's God-mother also, she called to ask him if he had been aware that the pastor, Elder Logan had called a special business meeting that evening, to which Louis responded he was not, she asked if anyone had called to tell him that someone had been dis-fellowshipped from the church, which he told her nobody had called him, that's when she dropped the big one, and told Louis, that he, Carol and the boys had all been put out of the church, Louis told her that he would get back with her later. He hung up with her, he immediately called his parents, and he asked his mom, and she told him that yes, that was what had gone on at the special meeting.

The following morning, Louis, Carol and the children, did take off for the four hour drive to the amusement park, they only stayed three days though, it was a vacation that seemed to be overshadowed with a thick dark cloud, so much was on his mind now, and he wanted to get back so that he wouldn't miss any of the services that were being held for Rod.

Upon returning home, Rod's old girlfriend Amber called Louis, she said she had gone by the funeral home to view Rod's body, that this was the only way that she said she would believe it, if she were to see Rod for herself, she also told Louis that she had lived her life in fear these past couple of years because of Rod, she also told Louis she wanted to thank him for that infamous day that he had stopped by to walk her to the apartment, because she now knew that had it not been for him, that day Rod most certainly would have killed her and himself, and that for this, she was eternally grateful to him.

Rod's funeral was a very somber one, Louis felt that this was such a waste of life, after all Rod was still a very young man, only twenty something, the biggest portion of his life should have still been ahead of him.

Louis now had another will to now execute, Rod left him the apartment building, two cars, and a few other things. Louis had always tried to do the right things in life, so he told the attorneys to draw up all the necessary paperwork, to try and gain custody of Rod's daughter, Annie. After a long and expensive court battle, the attorney told Louis that the cost for this alone, had gotten out of hand and that they recommended against it, therefore Louis dropped this fight, the child ended up with her maternal uncle. Louis gave both of Rod's cars away, and listed the apartment building with a real estate company to sell.

That following week, Louis did visit that little church around the corner from him, the services were much more structured, their boys loved it, after a month, Louis, Carol and the boys decided to make this their new church home. However all was not well in paradise, too many things began to happen with Carol, that she had no explanation for. She also brought home a letter from her supervisor, she had only been working four hours a day, but those hours were now changing from 9:00 A.M. to 1:00 P.M., which had perfectly coincided with the boys school hours, to a new set of working hours, now from 1:00 P.M. to 5:00 P.M., Louis told her that he wanted to go up and meet with her supervisor himself, but at Carol's pleading he did not, he even told her that she could quit working, which she did not want to do this.

While visiting his parents one Saturday, Louis was discussing with them, how unfair he thought it was that he and his family had been put out of the church, his mother Edith told him that the best thing to do, instead of going on hearsay, was to call Elder Logan himself, so at his mother's urging, he did just that, Edith gave him the number, and he called him from right there that very evening. Upon reaching Elder Logan at his home, Louis told him that he was a little puzzled as to how all the circumstances had unfolded as to why he and his family had been dis-fel-lowshipped from the church, Louis reminded him that he knew the doc-trine of the church well, and that he had followed the church bi-laws as stated in the manual, by telling him that he would be attending another church that particular Sunday.

Elder Logan told him that all this was true, but according to those same church bi-laws, your pastor has to give you permission to visit another church, he told Louis that true enough, he had told him that he would be visiting another church, but he told Louis that he had never told him that he had his permission, In addition to this he told Louis, I have someone in authority over me also, and I did exactly what I was told to do by putting you and your family out of the church, it was nothing personal that I had against you he told Louis.

Louis, not wanting to be contentious, did however ask him about another couple who normally came to church two or three times a year, and was always recognized upon their arrival, Elder Logan told him that they always came to him and told him that they had been out because they were sick, Louis asked him did he really believe that, he said no, so Louis said, let me get this straight, if I had lied and told you I was out sick, then it would have been okay, and Elder Logan told him yes it would have, Louis thanked him for his time and the explanation and ended the conver-sation. Told you,

"CHURCH-FOLK SOME MESSED-UP FOLK"

Right or wrong there was much to be learned from all this, for Louis, as well as the rest of the church members. Church politics are not a good thing, and on the surface, when things appear to be all going okay, the inner workings are much more like cancer, and given free reign, selfish agendas will eventually come to the surface.

At the new church Louis and his family had began attending, they blended in really well, everyone was extremely friendly, the children liked the church even more than Louis and Carol did, services were not quite as charismatic as they had been accustomed to, and there was only one mid-week service, not three, as he had become accustomed to at the other church, service times also, were now cut in half, in Louis's eyes, these were positive things.

That fall Louis received at work from Carol, she told him that Bishop Gray, the one who normally came into town to run a revival for me each year, was in town to run a revival for Elder Logan, and that he had called for Louis, saying that he would like to talk to him, she gave Louis the name and address to the hotel that he was staying at, and said that he had asked if Louis would stop up after he got off work to see him.

Louis now thought to himself, finally, the voice of reason, Louis had supposed within himself, that Bishop Gray had talked to Elder Logan, smoothed things out, and was now here to tell Louis that all parties con-cerned, now wanted him to come back and again be a part of their organi-zation, boy was he in for a rude awakening.

Upon leaving work, Louis went directly to the hotel to see Bishop Gray, they greeted one another and dispensed with all the formalities, discussed how much they each missed me, and then came the real reason Louis had been summoned up to the Bishop's hotel room. Bishop Gray explained to Louis, that he had also talked with me before I died, and that I had told him out of my own mouth, that I did not want Louis to give anyone in that organization anything of mine, he then went on to explain to Louis, that I had become senile in my old age, and that I did not realize what I was saying, Louis thought to himself, that it had been years since I had had my will drawn up and given him certain instructions on how to carry on, but these thoughts he kept to himself while Bishop Gray went on explain-ing the reason for his visit.

It all boiled down to this one thing, after listening to a quite lengthy display of his oratorical skills, Bishop Gray finally told him that the Lord had spoken to him, and told him to call Louis up to his room to talk to him, to tell him that the Lord wanted Louis to give Bishop Gray fifteen-thousand dollars, this was his sole purpose for wanting to talk to Louis, didn't I tell you,

"CHURCH-FOLK SOME MESSED-UP FOLK"

Not only was Louis totally shocked, he was also speechless, this isn't what he expected at all, where was this mans concern for a soul that might get lost in all this, for the desire to see reconciliation in situations of misunderstanding, the compassion for the babes in Christ, who might go back out and get entangled again into an ugly world of sin, it had all been clouded over by greed for the almighty dollar.

How pathetic, we, as individuals have become, again, we blame the Lord, How loosely we throw that phrase around, the Lord told me, most church-folk wouldn't know the voice of the Lord if he would speak to them.

1st Timothy 6:10

"For the love of money is the root of all evil."

The fact that Louis had left the church, never came up, and although he had heard things about Bishop Gray before, he had never really given it much thought, until one day while the three of us were sitting in my apartment, and Bishop Gray asked me if the Simeon in the book of Genesis 29:32, Jacob's son, and the Simeon in the book of Luke 2:25, were the same, this really made Louis wonder about a man like him being a Bishop and Pastor, but still Louis overlooked it.

I was however, very pleased with the answer that Louis gave him concerning the money, he looked Bishop Gray square in the eyes, and he said to him, did the Lord really tell you, to tell me, to give you fifteen-thousand dollars, with great anticipation he said, he most certainly did, to which Louis replied, well when the Lord tells me, then I'll give it to you, Louis then turned and left.

Upon arriving home, Louis told Carol what had went on, she said that she really wasn't that surprised, she said that it was a shame what people would do for the love of money, she also asked Louis did he think he should give Bishop Gray anything, he asked her what she thought, well she said, if God really told him to ask you, I think you should, well Louis said, how do we really know that God told him, and he ended that discussion. Also, he never did receive another call from Bishop Gray.

Proverbs 23:21

"For the drunkard and the glutton shall come to poverty: and drowsiness shall clothe a man with rags."

Money is one of the things that Louis, and his sister Delilah had been discussing earlier, when talking about discipline among ministers. The other thing that they were discussing was gluttony, one of the few things that are not taught on enough in our churches today, one of the points that Delilah wanted to convey, was how can a big three hundred pound minister, stand in the pulpit and teach me about discipline, and self denial, when it is quite obvious that he himself, lacks discipline in some area, we must be aware that in the fitness centered culture that we live in, this is most noticeable.

7

"A THREEFOLD CORD IS BROKEN"

Ecclesiastes 4:12

"And if one prevail against him, two shall withstand him, and a threefold cord is not quickly broken."

Although a threefold cord is not quickly broken, they can break, put enough pressure on anything and it will tend to buckle beneath the load. Its been said that death comes in three's, and for any man to lose three men in his lifetime, who were as close to him as these three were, in such a short time, can be life altering.

It was also about this time, that Louis received a call from his mother Edith, it was concerning his brother Rod, if you will remember, Rod, for most of his life, had been unwilling to work, therefore he had never had much throughout his life, and if for some reason his wife Donna, would give him money to pay the bills, they never would get paid, but the money would always end up disappearing, but she continued to try and trust him.

This last time that she had trusted him, their rent was already a month behind, and she, thinking that he would certainly know the consequences if he didn't pay it this month, entrusted the rent money to him again, to do this one small necessary task, and again he had failed, he had blown the money, and they were now being evicted within the next twenty-four hours.

Trust is something that an individual has to earn, by proving oneself to be trustworthy, it can't be forced on a person, the only thing you will gain by trying to force someone to be trustworthy, is disappointment.

Now keep in mind that when Rod, Louis's cousin had died, he had left Louis an apartment building, and although Louis had put it up for sale, it had not sold, so when Edith Timm's called Louis later that day, her first question was, are any of the suite's empty in your apartment building? naturally curious, Louis asked her why, and she went on to explain the dilemma that Rod had put himself into, Louis went on to tell her that she knew, if he allowed Rod and his wife to move into this building, that she knew that he would never get one penny in rent, to which Edith went on to explain, in true motherly fashion, well if no one is in there now, how much are you getting in rent, she went on to explain to Louis, that Rod was his brother and that if nothing else, it would be a sin to allow your own brother to be set out on the streets, while you had an empty apartment, oh the guilt that he felt.

Louis did allow his brother Rod to move into the empty apartment, against his better judgment, and there were many things that were going on in Rod's life, that later made Louis glad that he did allow him to move in.

Before anything else occurred, Louis said that he wanted to talk to Rod and his wife Donna, you know, sort of like a pep talk, to let them know that he expected the rent to be paid when it was due each month, and that the only reason that he was doing this, was because of their mother Edith. Rod's wife assured him that they would make sure that he got his rent every month, and on time. Rod and Donna did move in, and the first couple of months, everything went pretty good.

One day while Louis and Rod were at their parents home, Rod told his mother to feel his scalp, which she did, and she asked him had he been hit in the head by someone, she said she thought she felt a knot, Rod then pulled off his shirt, and there were big knots all over his back, he said that they had began popping up about six months before, he had not said anything, but know that they had began popping up on his head, he had become worried. At his mother Edith's urging, he called and made a doctors appointment.

The following week, Rod did go to the doctor, upon running all sorts of routine tests, and giving him a thorough physical examination, they told him that they would get back with him with the results by the end of the week. Rod left the hospital and went home, he had never been one to take very good care of himself, even this did not change that. Before that week was up, the hospital did call Rod, they told him that it was very important that they set up another appointment to see him again, as soon as possible, Rod told them that he would come in that following morning. The following morning Rod got up and got dressed, and he was at the hospital by 10:00 A.M.

There at the hospital, they set up an hour of orientation time, where they told Rod that he had an acute case of cancer of the lymph nodes, Rod did not understand the seriousness of this, and he asked them what could they do for it. This now entailed a barrage of questions and other tests, still Rod did not quite understand the seriousness of the matter. After all, he thought to himself, I'm only thirty-four years old, they'll cure me, and once again all will be well.

First of all, had he gone to the doctor when he first realized something was wrong, if something can be done at all, there would have been a much better chance of doing when you catch these problems at the very beginning. The doctors explained to him that at this point, they wanted to immediately start him off with mild form of chemotherapy, from there they would increase it as time progressed. After the first month, Rod was admitted into the hospital, with some minor complications, he was only there ten days before they released him, still, he did nothing to take care of himself.

Rod's primary care physician, had set up appointments for him to come into the hospital for chemotherapy treatments every Friday. Rod started the first two weeks off fine, then he'd skip a week, then he'd skip two weeks, then three, till finally the doctors got fed up with him, and told him that he didn't think Rod really cared, whether he lived or not himself. Rod did care, but like many of us, we've never died before, so we don't really comprehend the finality of it, and Rod, again like many of us, just figured, I'll be alright, I'm a young man, it's just not my time yet. Contrary to what we may think, we do not control our own destiny:

Psalm 100:3

"Know ye that the Lord he is God: it is he that hath made us, and not we ourselves; we are his people, and the sheep of his pasture.

As time progressed, Rod's bouts of sickness became much more frequent, on several of what were supposed to be his outpatient visits, he was admitted, and would remain a patient, often from four to six days at a time. The more tests that the doctors ran, the more obvious it became to them that the prognosis was not looking too good, but try as they may, they just could not seem to get this through to Rod.

Louis, in light of Rod's condition was much more compassionate with him now, he had always made sure when he had to go over to the apartment for anything, that he would make sure to stop and visit with Rod for a while. For the most part, Donna would make sure to get the rent money to Louis, but he had already purposed in his heart, that if something came up and they did not offer it to him, that he would not ask for it.

Death seems to draw out the best and the worse in individuals, most families, however tension filled they may be, death seems to break down some of the barriers. It doesn't really matter what has gone on, all that you can think about in these crucial times is that we are all a family, and all of those little grudges, that we seemed to have magnified in this life, now begin to seem so minute, we begin to see our own folly in such matters, we finally begin to realize that God is much more concerned with people, than he is with things.

St. John 3:16

"For God so loved the world, that he gave his only begotten Son, that whosoever believeth in him should not perish, but have everlasting life"

When the bible talks about God so loving the world, this encompasses the world of lost individuals, not things, things are the least of God's concerns, it is those lost souls that he shed his innocent blood for, it is these lost souls, that the very heart of God is pleading and battling for, those souls that just don't seem to understand, that if we are not wise in our choices today, we will have an eternity to regret it.

Rod's last bout in the hospital, was probably his worst one. This time, because the cancer was in such an advanced stage, the doctors felt that they wanted to try something new, their feelings being, that they had nothing to lose, well Rod had nothing to gain, their new procedures, did nothing to stop the cancer from spreading. Although on the exterior, Rod still looked okay, and his mind was still sharp, internal tests that were ran, showed that he probably had, only a matter of weeks to live, even in the light of news like this, we are sometimes in denial, yes God can heal, he is still in the miracle working business, but all do not receive a miracle, all do not receive healing.

Rod was now approaching his third week in the hospital, Louis would go out every Sunday after church and spend the remainder of his afternoon with Rod, many of their other family members would do the same. The cancer did not eat away at Rod, as it does many people, all of his deterioration, seemed to be internally, at the onset of this horrific disease, he weighed in at one-hundred and eighty-five pounds, today he weighed in, and he was still at the exact same weight.

As week four approached, the doctors said that they had exhausted all of their resources, and that there was nothing more that they could do, it was out of their hands. When Louis went to see Rod that fourth week, he did not look as good, however he still had his sense of humor, Rod said to Louis, watch this, he then pressed the buzzer for a nurse, when she answered, he said help me, I've fallen and I can't get up, then he would just crack himself up laughing, still not understanding the brevity of his own life. Louis would always pray with him, and ask him if he had gotten things right with God, Rod said he had, but Louis would still lead him in the sinners prayer, always telling him to repeat these words and mean it,

> *"Lord Jesus, forgive me for my sins, I believe that you died to take away the sins of the world, that you rose from the grave with all power, and that without you, I cannot be saved, I ask you right now to come into my heart and take up residence, rest, rule and abide with me, I accept you as my personal Lord and Savior".*

Louis left that evening, not knowing that this would be the last time that he would ever have a conversation with Rod. About the middle of the following week, the doctors there told Rod that they would probably be discharging him in a couple of days, and that they would set up an appointment for him, for a consultation with a representative from hospice.

Rod called his wife Donna, to tell her what the doctors were planning, and to his surprise, she asked him if they discharged him, where would he be going, she told him that he had not been the kind of husband that deserved to have her take care of him, therefore she said that he was not coming there. Rod called and told his mother Edith about the conversation he had just had with his wife, and in a true motherly fashion, she told him that he could come to her house, that she would take it upon herself to care for him.

Edith Timm's called the hospice hotline herself the following morning, she spoke with someone, who then directed her to the correct person, and there she explained the situation, she also informed them that she was Rod's mother, and that he would be coming to live with her, upon his release from the hospital. Edith had not been in the best of shape herself, she had gone through an extremely delicate surgery a few years prior to this, from which she had never totally recovered, and in addition to this she still worked a full time job.

But first and foremost, she was a mother, and her logic was, that if God brings you to it, that same God will bring you through it, she said that she did not know how she would manage all this, but she also said that I serve a risen Saviour, and I know that the Lord will make a way.

The hospice representative called the Timm's home that Friday, they spoke with Edith, they told her that the medical equipment company would be bringing out a hospital bed and a port-a-pot that Saturday, and they also asked her if there was anything else that she could think of that she needed, which she said that she could not. The following day, the medical equipment company arrived, and they did just as they had said, they delivered and set up those items, right in the Timm's family room.

Donna, Rod's wife, also called Edith that Saturday evening, she explained that she had enough on her already, and that she just couldn't take care of a sick man right now, she wasn't trying to be mean or anything, but he had just not been a good husband to her and that nobody knew what he had taken her through, Edith told Donna that she understood exactly where she was coming from, that she knew her son, and that he had never been a responsible type person, but she also said to Donna, you knew all of that when you married him, to which Donna said, she did.

The following day, Louis went to the hospital as usual to visit Rod, but his Sunday things were different, Rod was not coherent, he looked different, much darker than normal, Louis went over and opened his eyelid, even the white in his eyes were now darkly discolored, Louis tried talking to Rod, but it was as if he wanted to respond, but just couldn't. Louis stayed a while, then he prayed for him and left. It was a good thirty to forty-five minute ride home for Louis, and the image of Rod laying there, weighed very heavily on him.

Upon arriving home, Carol told him that the hospital had just called all of the family members, and told them that they would suggest that all of the immediate family get there as soon as possible. Louis got back in his car and raced back to the hospital, upon arriving and getting off the elevator, he saw two of his sisters standing outside of Rod's hospital room crying, and as he walked towards them they said, he's dead, and they began to cry even harder.

This was the closest to home, that death had ever hit this family, and they were not handling it well, not well at all. Edith took it the worst, she said that there is just something embedded in our internal make-up, that just says that a child should not die before the parent, this is only something that a parent, who has lost a child can understand, she had prayed and fasted, all to no avail, however, she had the blessed assurance, that through it all, God knew what was best.

Now in telling about Rod, this all goes back to church-folk, now let me explain.

Now remember, Rod is the one that had said God wanted him to be a preacher during the great tribulation period, which again goes back to people blaming God for the things that they themselves want to justify. In the times of the prophets, you only had to prophesy one thing that did not come to pass, to be labeled a false prophet. Now if God had really wanted Rod to be a preacher during the great tribulation period, and had also made this known to Rod, would he really be lying there in the hospital dead, absolutely not. Still,

"CHURCH-FOLK SOME MESSED-UP FOLK"

What we are now doing is nothing new, we want to continually excuse and minimize our own sins and shortcomings, all the while magnifying those of others, all of God's promises are true, the good and the bad, he is a God of love, but he is also a God of wrath:

Hebrews 12:29

"For our God is a consuming fire."

We must not continue to blame God when we fall short, there is no failure in God. I love the Lord, but I also love to sin, however, my Love for God, far outweighs my love to sin,

"Two natures fight—within my breast
One is cursed—the other is blessed
The one I love—the other I hate
The one that I let rule—will dominate"

This all goes back to choices, we can find an excuse to do anything that we choose to do, an excuse, is nothing more than a sick reason. God has not raised his standards, we have lowered ours, what we found shockingly disgusting, and utterly amazing fifty years ago, now seems to be amusing to the masses.

Hebrews 13:8

"Jesus Christ the same yesterday, and to day, and for ever."

God hasn't changed we have, we have become spoiled with our own sins,

Romans 3:23

"For all have sinned, and come short of the glory of God."

This goes for me, just as it does for you.

Ezekiel 18:4

"Behold, all souls are mine; as the soul of the father, so also the soul of the son is mine: the soul that sinneth, it shall die."

He didn't say might die, there is no two ways about this, and there is no way around it, we may as well come clean with God.

Hebrews 2:3

"How shall we escape, if we neglect so great salvation; which at the first began to be spoken by the Lord, and was confirmed unto us by them that heard him."

We shall not escape, contrary to what some might say. When the Lord Jesus comes back, I can assure you that it will not be to do his first work all over again, he is coming back for a prepared people, to take them to a prepared place, don't let it be said too late for us, we are in the dressing room of life right now, and if we are not properly dressed upon the second coming of our Lord and Saviour, Jesus Christ, we will not have the time to get dressed when he arrives.

Ephesians 5:27

*"That he might present it to himself a glorious church, not having spot, or wrinkle, or any such thing; but that it should be holy and without **blemish**."*

Only those, who's sins have been washed white in the blood of the Lamb, will he take with him, we must all be about our fathers business, for none but the righteous, shall be saved and see God, in all of his glory, splendor and majesty, the Lord is getting us ready for that great day.

This was the close of yet another chapter in Louis's life, some things there is just no being prepared for.

8

"THE CALM BEFORE THE STORM"

2 Thessalonians 5:3

"For when they shall say, Peace and safety; then sudden destruction cometh upon them, as travail upon a woman with child; and they shall not escape."

With the death of his brother Rod, and the funeral behind him, Louis wanted to now get on with the rest of his life, and what a life it would turn out to be for him.

Louis and Carol had now settled into the new church, and on the surface, everything appeared to be going along pretty smooth, the two of them had a pretty good relationship with the Pastor and his wife there, and the entire church seemed to welcome them in.

As far as work goes, Louis loved what he was doing now, and it seemed that his life was now headed in a direction, that most people only dreamed of. In these past ten years, he had really grown to love his wife and children, and the responsibility of providing for them, brought him great joy and an unequaled satisfaction, along with these, he now felt a sense of completeness. Junior and Byron, looked up to their dad, and had the utmost respect for him, and the four of them had an excellent relationship.

Louis would often tell some of his co-workers that had met Carol, to take a good look at her, he said that his wife was the closest thing to an angel, that most of them would ever come into contact with. Louis was not the first man to feel this way about his wife, neither was he the first man that would ever be disappointed by his wife.

One of the things that had weighed heavily on Louis's mind, was that before their boys got into middle school, that he would like to buy another house for his family, just to put them into a better school system. He would look at suburban homes periodically, just to get a feel for what was out there, he often prayed that in this venture, the Lord would direct him.

At this new church, because of some of the experiences he had had in the past, he was very careful not to take on too much responsibility, nor try to form too close a relationship with anyone, however, whenever a need would arise, he was always willing to lend a helping hand. This also helped him to get to know the other church members a little better.

This particular year Louis had also loaned an Elder of a church, a substantial sum of money for a business venture that he was pursuing, and things were not going very good in that respect, he had began compiling a list of the people that owed him, it was quite lengthy, and would continue to grow from this point on.

Something that Louis had purposed in his heart was, that the money I had left for him, he would take it, and put it in a special account, not to be bothered, and it would always be there as sort of a buffer, which was probably one of the wisest things that he, as a young man did in his entire lifetime. How many of us have seen loved ones come into money, or have come into it ourselves for that matter, only to squander it foolishly on unnecessary things, then wonder where it went.

There are times in an individuals life, where they will only get a one shot deal like this, once in their entire life, only to blow it, and for the rest of their life, they think, only if this could happen once again, they will say to themselves and even to others at times, this time I'd be much wiser with it, I'd save some for a rainy day, I'd give some to the church, only if.

Well friends, most of the time, we simply do not get a second chance, you know the old saying, that you never get a second chance, to make a good first impression, how many of us do the same exact thing with God, we blow off our chances now, to have a right relationship with him, and squander our lives away, but when he returns to take up his church, when we stand before him in judgment, there will be no second chances,

Malachi 3:17

"And they shall be mine, saith the LORD of hosts, in that day when I make up my jewels; and I will spare them, as a man spareth his own son that serveth him."

Romans 14:10

"But why dost thou judge thy brother? or why dost thou set at nought thy brother? for we shall all stand before the judgment seat of Christ."

2 Corinthians 5:10

"For we must all appear before the judgment seat of Christ; that every one may receive the things done in his body, according to that he hath done, whether it be good or bad."

As a child, Louis had made it up in his mind, that he wanted to please God, no matter what the cost was, and all of the negative things that now had happened in his life, he counted them as valuable growing and learning experiences.

One of the things that had troubled Louis on occasion, was the fact that as a teenager, he had been very promiscuous sexually, he, like most of you, knew what the word of God's word said regarding this, but like many others, he had gone contrary to the word and to the will of God concerning this area. The word of God says that we are to keep ourselves pure,

1 Thessalonians 4:3

"For this is the will of God, even your sanctification, that you should abstain from fornication: That everyone of you should know how to possess his vessel in sanctification and honour; Not in the lust of concupiscence, even as the gentiles which know not God."

The lesson that Louis had learned from all of his own shortcomings in this area was this, that of the many opportunities that presented themselves for him to stray outside of the boundaries of his marriage vows, had he not been so promiscuous as a teenager, the curiosity of it all, would have no doubt gotten the best of him, and he would have succumbed to many of these illicit temptations that had been set before him.

Carol had a girlfriend whom she had known since she was about ten years old named Brenda, Brenda had gotten together with Rich at the tender age of about fourteen, they had married at twenty, and had four children by the time they were twenty-eight. While Louis and Carol were talking one day, Carol told him that Brenda had confided in her, that Rich was the only man that she had ever been intimate with, and for that matter, the only man that she had ever even been out with, and she now found herself with this burning desire, to have an experience with someone other than Rich, now with that kind of curiosity, what do most of you think will eventually happen.

1 John 5:17

"All unrighteousness is sin: and there is a sin not unto death."

The bible is God's infallible word, and the same principles that he established in the beginning of time, they still apply today, I'm not asking anyone to agree, or disagree with me, I'm simply stating my feelings as a man, trying to choose between the lesser of two evils, I would much rather marry a woman who has had her indiscretions before I married her, as opposed to me marrying a lily white bride, only for her to have these indiscretions after I marry her, personally I don't believe I would be as forgiving. It is without a doubt better to contain yourself, the great apostle Paul said himself:

1 Corinthians 7:9

"But if they cannot contain, let them marry; for it is better to marry than to burn."

One thing I would like you to keep in mind, is that fornication involves only two individuals, adultery involves three, and sometimes four, aside from involving God, and just in case you're wondering, yes Brenda is church-folk, and

"CHURCH-FOLK SOME MESSED-UP FOLK"

One Thursday that same fall, Louis received the scare of his life, Carol would normally pick the boys up from the sitter, and be home by about 5:15 P.M., this particular day, 5:45 P.M. had rolled around and they still were not at home, and Louis had not heard neither hide nor hair from them, Louis figured that Carol had probably picked the boys up and gone to the store or something, but he said to himself, I'll call the sitter just to make sure, he called and the sitter said that the boys were still there, and that she had also began to worry, because this just wasn't like Carol. Louis went over and picked the boys up, he then returned home and called Carol's job, he was told that Carol was scheduled off that day, which totally caught him off guard, he thought he always knew when she was off.

His mind began racing, all of the normal what ifs that crosses a persons mind in situations like this crossed his, he called her parents, they had not heard a thing, now they had began to worry also. As Louis sat there, worried half out of his mind with fear, having exhausted all possible avenues, the telephone rang, it was now about 8:00 P.M., and it was Carol on the other end, she said that she had just gone out driving to clear her head and that the time had gotten away from her, Louis told her that she could come and get her clothes and get out, he told her that he refused to continually go through this with her.

You see on several other occasions, when Carol could not have her own way, she would run off to her parents home and stay, sometimes a day, or a week, sometimes up to two weeks long, however the last time that she had left him, Louis told her that if she ever left again, he would not allow her to return again.

Louis sat there, staring out of the living room window, he was livid. After about forty-five minutes had gone by, he saw her pulling up the long driveway to their home with her parents following close behind her in their vehicle. Carol waited while her parents got out of their car, and the three of them came into the house together. Louis did not try in any way to conceal his anger, he told her right there in front of both her parents, that as far as he was concerned, she could feel free to take whatever it was that she wanted to take, and leave the premises that night for good, Carol explained to Louis, that this was not what she wanted to do at all, she said that all she wanted to do, was to feel like she contributed more to their relationship than she did, that she had always wanted more of a career than she now had.

Carol confided to Louis that she had always wanted to go back to school, and that she just thought that he would not allow her to, her father even asked Louis, what harm would it be if she wanted to go and take a few classes, Louis told him that he didn't see any harm in it at all, that he himself had suggested that before to Carol. After talking for about an hour, Louis felt somewhat better, and at Carol's fathers urging, Louis agreed to put all of this behind them, and to go on from here, however he was still very angry, and this was not the end of this, trust me.

Their neighborhood also, in just the short ten years or so that they had been there, had changed tremendously, one night Louis arrived home late, during a terrible thunderstorm. While riding down the street, as he approached his driveway, he saw a naked man, stumbling down the sidewalk, he immediately went into the house and called the authorities, these were the kind of things that Louis took note of and pondered them in his heart, a real man is not looking out so much for his own well being, but more so for the safety of his family, this is the true mans first priority.

Now back to the church that Louis was now attending, unknown to Louis, Pastor Platt had been exploring the possibility of relocating also, the demographics in the area in which he lived had also changed, and he wanted out, just like Louis, before things got any worse, you see he also had two small children, and like most any pastor would do, he kept the fact that he had been looking to move elsewhere kind of quiet. For the most part, most pastors will not just up and leave without having something else lined up for themselves, they become very dependent on that extra income.

The longer Louis and Carol were at the church now, the more comfortable the four of them became there, his main concern in a church, was that the unadulterated word of God be taught in word and example, most of the other things he could overlook, but he would often ask Carol and the boys, out of concern for them, if they were okay there, they always assured him that they were.

They also found out that one of the women there at the church, that they had befriended was a real estate agent, this also prompted him to began looking a little more seriously for another home to purchase, Louis had usually shied away from working with real estate agents, he did not want to feel obligated to do business with them, or for them to feel he was obligated to them, this agent was willing to follow his lead.

Louis on one hand was and always had been very conservative, but there were certain things that he did indulge himself in, and when he did, he made sure that he bought the very best, he made pretty good money, and for the most part he was very well disciplined with it. According to the word of God, there is nothing wrong with enjoying that which we have worked for with our own hands, some may even try to put you on a guilt trip about it, I say if God doesn't condemn you for it, please don't let anybody else do it:

Ecclesiastes 5:18

"Behold that which I have seen: it is good and comely for one to eat and to drink, and to enjoy the good of all his labour that he taketh under the sun all the days of his life, which God giveth him; for it is his portion."

Louis had always tried to not live just for the here and now, but for the many out there that would say that tomorrow is not promised to you, so I'm going to enjoy what I have right now. Louis would often think to himself, well just in case I do make it until tomorrow, I'm going to save a little, he would often tell his countless family members, that if you own a house or a car, you need to have a little savings just in case one or the other needs some unplanned for repairs, because sooner or later, one of them will.

This reminds me of a telephone call that Louis received at work one morning about 9:30 A.M., it was Carol, telling him that she was on her way home from visiting with her mother, and that about half way home the car had stopped, Louis called a tow truck and had it towed to a shop where it was discovered that the transmission had gone bad, Louis told them whatever the charge was, go ahead and repair it and he would settle up with them at the appointed time of pick up.

Because of Louis's love for exotic automobiles, he subscribed to several worldwide automobile magazines, it was also about this same time, that he had seen an ad at an out of state automobile dealership, it seemed to him that they had some extremely reasonable prices on just the type of automobiles that he liked, he showed the magazine to Carol and said, how about we fly down there, check these cars out and make it a weekend getaway, Carol was in agreement.

Louis made all of the necessary reservations, dropped the boys off at one of their sisters house, and from there they headed for the airport. He had been on an airplane before, but looking at Carol, hoping that she wouldn't be too afraid, he assured her that he had flown before and there was nothing for her to fear, that the flight would be fine, and that after her first flight, she would not want to travel any other way.

After arriving at their appointed designation, they checked into a hotel, where Louis also got directions to the automobile dealership. Later that afternoon they went to the dealership, looked around for quite a long while, and Louis picked out four cars that he told them he wanted to purchase, he worked out the deal with the owner, got all the preliminaries out of the way, told them where to ship the cars and prepared to leave, just then a car hauler pulled in, loaded with more cars that caught the attention of Louis, as he watched them being unloaded, he walked back into the dealership and bought three of them also, for a total of seven cars.

Never mind the fact that he already had five cars at home. Although Louis was looking at this as a business venture, others thought that this was a bit excessive. All seven of the cars arrived on a truck, one week later, Louis ran an ad in the local classifieds, he sold all seven cars, got all of his money back, plus a little extra for all his time and effort, most of all, he enjoyed it.

He and Carol also began going to open houses, most of them he would see in the local newspaper, not wanting to tie up an agents time, he told the woman that was an agent at his new church, that they had been going out looking at houses, and that if they found something that they really liked, that he would then contact her and steer the deal her way, he assured her that knew exactly what he was doing, you see this is what he had gone to college for when he first graduated from high school, his original plan had been, to be a real estate agent, invest in property and make a ton of money doing this, however after owning two apartment buildings and three homes, and this alone was enough to let him know that this was not what he really wanted to do in life.

It took six months, but Louis and Carol finally found the perfect home, it was everything that you could ask for in a home, far above anything that Louis had ever imagined as a child. He called the woman at the church and told her about it, she set up an appointment for them to view it, and Louis and Carol did purchase that very home. The home had been previously owned by a doctor and his family, and had been remodeled to absolute perfection, the home didn't need a thing, he was in negotiations for more than two weeks concerning it, but it saved him nearly twenty-five percent off of the original asking price, Carol was not quite as enthused as Louis was, but then she had a different agenda from him, as you'll later see.

That following month, Pastor Platt finally announced to the entire congregation that he and his family would be relocating and leaving the church within the next thirty days, thus leaving the church in desperate need of a Pastor. This sort of caught everyone off guard. There is, and always has been a shortage of good, Godly, dedicated pastors, who are willing to be led by the spirit of God. At the end of the appointed time which he had specified, Pastor Platt did leave, it was the week after Louis and Carol had moved into their new home, Pastor Platt was able to come over and pray for and bless their new home.

The week after Pastor Platt left, Louis volunteered to preach the Sunday morning service, this was his first sermon, the new pastor wasn't scheduled to start until the following Sunday, after Louis preached, many in the congregation told him, that had they known he had it in him, they would have asked him to be the new pastor, however, it was not God's time for Louis to exercise his gift, and he was never one to run out ahead of God, please remember, that timing is everything.

Also that same Sunday, the church council members ran copies of the new incoming pastors resume, they passed them out to all the members that were present, this man sure made himself sound good. We must remember this, that pastors are people first, and we should not be surprised if and when they want to build themselves up, because according to his resume, he had been the pastor of a fairly large church, with nearly two-hundred members under him, whereas in actuality, he was in a small storefront with five members, as time would later reveal.

Unfortunately, church-folk are some of the most trusting and naïve people that there are, one reason is that instead of studying the word of God for themselves, they rely solely on the preachers to convey the word to them in an honest and forthright method, hoping that they will not only know the way, and show the way, but that most importantly, they will go the way themselves, this is not always the way it's done though;

2 Timothy 2:15

"Study to show thyself approved unto God, a workman that needeth not be ashamed, rightly dividing the word of truth."

The call of God into the ministry, is no longer a calling, it has now become an occupation, this, God is not pleased with at all, every man has gone after his own way, what God is and always has been looking for, are those individuals that have a genuine concern not only for God, but also for lost souls, with no self seeking motives.

We must at all cost remember, that others may see what we do, but God sees why we do it. The only reward some people will ever receive, will be what they can con out of people right here in this present world, God's eyes are not closed to these kinds of things that go on, but he is longsuffering, hoping that we will all see the error of our way, before its too late;

Haggai 1:5

"Now therefore thus saith the Lord of hosts; Consider your ways."

As time has progressed, it seems that more and more, preachers are concerned more with the power, the prestige and the position, than they are with actually the saving of souls, there are many ministers out there today, that will not sit under good sound doctrine long enough to learn the bible themselves, let alone be able to teach it to others, instead, desiring to be pastors, many have gone out and started up a church of their own somewhere, just to be able to say that they are the pastor, they think that this sounds prestigious to others, never thinking about how it sounds to God, this is whom we should really be trying to please anyway, if God is not the head of it, and we start anything without his divine blessing, we start out with a problem, it doesn't really matter if it looks okay to man or not, most times, even man is not fooled.

The following Sunday, the new pastor arrived there to shepherd the members, his name was Carl Evans, he had a wife and one teenage son, the entire church was very warm and receptive to the entire family, and from the very onset, it all seemed to be a very smooth transition. Upon his arrival, the congregation immediately began to grow, and so did the finances of the church, which now meant that many of the outreach ministries could now be expanded. Pastor Evans dove right in, and he worked very diligently in and around the church, something many pastors do not believe that they should have to do.

The first year that he was there all went very well, many of the members volunteered to fill positions in the church as they were needed, the first Saturday of each month was designated clean up day, most Saturdays, more people would show up to clean the church, than was actually needed. What I have also noticed is that up until some shortcomings are identified in a leader or pastor, the people are usually more than willing to sacrifice of their time and of their monies for the up building of the church, but once these shortcomings are identified, whether they are real or imagined, the people will quickly freeze up, not only on the pastor, but many times on God also. The apostle Paul said that we must be discreet;

Ephesians 5:15

"See then that ye walk circumspectly, not as fools, but as wise."

Many individuals are looking at the preacher/pastor or leader, almost in the place of God, and when he or she fails in some area of their lives, or some weakness becomes known, we must know that there are a countless number of individuals, whose faith will now be tested and shaken;

2 Corinthians 3:2

"Ye are our epistle written in our hearts, known and read of all men."

God loves all of his creation, and it breaks his heart, when we continually fail to yield our members to him, and him alone, payday will come, our God is too wise to make a mistake, and he is too righteous to be unjust, in his infinite wisdom, he allows us to make our own choices, and to enjoy sin for a season, only to graciously accept us upon our return to him.

The first year that Louis and Carol were in their new home, it was absolutely beautiful, it was as if the divine hand of God had really been gracious to the both of them, not only the home, Louis also went out and purchased for the family, a new Lincoln Continental that same month. Now on the exterior, it seemed as if life was almost perfect for the two of them right now. The boys were now in a new school system, which was one of Louis's original concerns, it seemed like both he and Carol's jobs were going well, Louis thanked God continuously and thought to himself, what more could a man ask for, the Lord has given me the very desires of my heart, what a mighty God we serve.

Psalms 37:4

"Delight thyself also in the Lord; and he shall give thee the desires of thine heart."

Louis took Carol to an expensive furniture store, they picked out all new furniture, very nice stuff. He even went out and upgraded Carol's wedding ring, this was the third set that he had purchased for her.

Proverbs 13:22

"A good man leaveth an inheritance to his children's children: and the wealth of the sinner is laid up for the just."

Louis had befriended a local millionaire a couple of years before my death. Most of the people that would come into contact with Louis liked him very much, he was normally a very pleasant personable person, knowledgeable in many areas, and he never asked or expected anything from anyone, he had always been willing to work for whatever it was that he wanted, and things were no different now.

Many of the people that Louis met, would just call him when they wanted someone to talk to, one individual told him that he had no idea how hard it was just to find someone to talk to with common sense, someone that was able to hold an intelligent conversation, so it was with this local millionaire, he would just call Louis sometimes, once he called and they got on the subject of Louis's new home, and how much he owed on it, this millionaire who's name was Roe, told Louis to come out to is house and pick a check up to pay it off, Louis and Carol got in the car and drove over to see him, where he wrote Louis out a check, which Louis then promptly took to the bank, and their new home was paid for, free and clear, eight months after they moved into it, now tell me, who wouldn't serve a God like this.

The mind is a very powerful thing, and just as with the blessings of God, there are things that we just don't feel that we deserve, because we tend to feel that we are not coming up to the mark, when it comes to living our lives to please God, there are those that will unwittingly sabotage themselves, Louis once had a co-worker tell him, that according to the word of God, Jesus had promised that he would go and prepare a place for those that walk according to his statutes and commands,

St. John 14:2

"In my Father's house are many mansions: if it were not so, I would have told you. I go to prepare a place for you."

Well what this co-worker told Louis was, that I know that I'm missing the mark, therefore I'm not really expecting a mansion, I'm only expecting a split level. Louis said that he wanted everything that God had promised him, even the mansion. This is the exact mentality, that just as that co-worker, many of us have today, well, I know I'm not what I should be, but I'm better than some folks I know, tell me then, why aren't you what you should be?, because too many of us are using the wrong measuring stick for our lives,

1ˢᵗ Corinthians 11:1

"Be ye followers of me, even as I also am of Christ."

Psalm 37:37

"Mark the perfect man, and behold the upright: for the end of that man is peace."

Its okay to look at someone with admiration, to even desire to be like them in certain ways, ways that are pertaining to godliness and holiness, but as the great apostle Paul told the church at Corinth above, we must follow an individual only to the extent that the individual is setting a Christ like example in his or her life. If we want to be imitators of one who will not lead us astray, it is an absolute must that we follow a perfect and sinless individual as our example, that being only found in the person of Jesus Christ himself.

Matthew 19:17

"And he said unto him, Why callest thou me good? There is none good but one, that is, God: but if thou wilt enter into life, keep the commandments."

Colossians 2:9

"For in him dwelleth all the fullness of the Godhead bodily."

"If we are to imitate anyone, let it be Jesus"

He alone paid the price for all of our sins.

He alone rose walking in newness of life.

He alone has ascended into heaven.

He alone will come back as the final judge.

9

"THE EYE OF THE STORM"

1st Corinthians 15:58

"Therefore, my beloved brethren, be ye stedfast, unmoveable, always abounding in the work of the Lord, forasmuch as ye know that your labour is not in vain in the Lord."

2nd Corinthians 11:13-15

"For such are false apostles, deceitful workers, transforming themselves into the apostles of Christ. And no marvel; for Satan himself is transformed into an angel of light. Therefore it is no great thing if his ministers also be transformed as the ministers of righteousness; whose end shall be according to their works."

2nd Corinthians 13:5

"Examine yourselves, whether ye be in the faith; prove your own selves. Know ye not your own selves, how that Jesus Christ is in you, except ye be reprobates?"

Philippians 3:2

"Beware of dogs, beware of evil workers, beware of the concision."

Colossians 3:9

"Lie not one to another, seeing that ye have put off the old man with his deeds."

1st Thessalonians 5:17

"Pray without ceasing."

1st Thessalonians 5:22

"Abstain from all appearance of evil."

2nd Timothy 2:19

"Nevertheless the foundation of God standeth sure, having this seal, The Lord knoweth them that are his. And, let every one that nameth the name of Christ depart from iniquity."

2nd Timothy 3:5

"Having a form of godliness, but denying the power thereof: from such turn away."

Titus 1:2

"In hope of eternal life, which God, that cannot lie, promised before the world began."

Hebrews 10:23

"Let us hold fast the profession of our faith without wavering; (for he is faithful that promised)."

Hebrews 13:4

"Marriage is honourable in all, and the bed undefiled: but whore-mongers and adulterers God will judge."

1st Peter 3:12

"For the eyes of the Lord are over the righteous, and his ears are open unto their prayers: but the face of the Lord is against them that do evil."

1st Peter 4:12

"Beloved, think it not strange concerning the fiery trial which is to try you, as though some strange thing happened unto you."

1st Peter 4:18

"And if the righteous scarcely be saved, where shall the ungodly and the sinner appear?"

2nd Peter 1:10

"Wherefore the rather, brethren, give diligence to make your calling and election sure: for if ye do these things, ye shall never fall."

2nd Peter 2:4

"For if God spared not the angels that sinned, but cast them down to hell, and delivered them into chains of darkness, to be reserved unto judgment."

1st John 2:27

"But the anointing which ye have received of him abideth in you, and ye need not that any man teach you: but as the same anointing teacheth you of all things, and is truth, and is no lie, and even as it hath taught you, ye shall abide in him."

1st John 3:7

"Little children, let no man deceive you: he that doeth righteousness is righteous, even as he is righteous."

1st John 4:1

"Beloved, believe not every spirit, but try the spirits whether they are of God: because many false prophets are gone out into the world."

Revelation 9:6

"And in those days shall men seek death, and shall not find it; and shall desire to die, and death shall flee from them."

Not trying to inundate anyone with scripture, but these all are so appropriate to what went on in the next chapter of Louis's life, this was a time in his life, that if he could have done like Job, he would have cursed the day that he had been born, this was a time so devastating to him, that the very Angel's in heaven had to miraculously sustain him through the supernatural means of refreshing.

Acts 3:19

"Repent ye therefore, and be converted, that your sins may be blotted out, when the times of refreshing shall come from the presence of the Lord."

Louis and Carol's second year in their new home was not quite as exciting now, chinks had began to now appear in their armor, too many inexplicable occurrences began to happen, there had been too much lost time on Carol's account, that just could not be accounted for. In the majority of problem marriages, it has often been said, that in the event that an affair is going on, the spouse is always the last one to know, I beg to differ, the spouse is always the last one to accept and acknowledge these feelings, they are normally the first ones to know, they normally get some sort of tell-tell signs, upon which they usually began to suspect something, however what ultimately happens is, that in love, you want to give that significant other the benefit of the doubt, so blindly, we accept these half baked stories that they have concocted, whatever credibility they may have or lack.

We still have our gut feelings and instinct, and if either one of these tells us that something is wrong, ninety-five percent of the time there really is something wrong, do not disregard these feelings, even when your spouse adamantly tells you that its all in your mind, when someone is truly being faithful to someone, they don't mind giving an account of their time.

At the very beginning of that second year, Louis became very ill, he went to see several specialists, all of whom could really find nothing wrong, one of them had even suggested that he undergo some exploratory surgery, and even went so far as to set up an appointment and have it scheduled, he used some of the normal scare tactics of what could happen if it wasn't done, even so, Louis would not agree to this, he had began to develop severe nasal polyps, that had began to slowly suffocate him by blocking off his air passage, the doctors ran numerous tests, MRI's and cat scans, all to no avail, then Louis did the only thing that he could do, he stretched out on the Lord his God, and prayed for a healing, and God intervened, and he healed him of this condition completely.

Genesis 4:1

"And Adam knew Eve his wife; and she conceived, and bare Cain, and said, I have gotten a man from the Lord."

It was also about this time, that Louis had done a lot of soul searching over a matter from his past, really two matters from his past, and now he finally wanted some closure them. As discussed earlier, Louis had known his share of women, by this I mean knew in the biblical sense, and there was one in particular, that had a daughter that was now fourteen years old, whom he had always wondered if this could possibly be his child, although Francis, the girls mother had always assured him that she was not his daughter. Louis and Francis had grown up together, and as teenagers, they had both been very promiscuous, but they had always remained close friends, even a little more than friends at times, if you know what I mean.

When Francis became pregnant, they were only about sixteen years old, and Louis did not even find out that she was pregnant, until she was going into her fifth month, throughout her entire pregnancy they remained friends, Louis would often ask her if it was possible that he could be the father, and she would always assure him that he was not, she even told him the name of the child's father, it was another young man that he also knew well. As Francis's pregnancy had progressed, the two of them did not talk as much, mostly because Francis had become very evil during the last two to three months of her pregnancy, although the two of them did still see each other on a daily basis, you see they were still in high school at this time, the same high school mind you.

Even back then, Louis may have been a very young man, but he was still a determined young man, knowing that one day he wanted something more out of life, than he had right now, he had always worked, and for just about as long as he or I could remember, since about the age of twelve, and things were no different now, he was still working. During his high school years, he worked at a small hospital not far from his families home, but because he was still in high school, he worked mostly evenings and week-ends, still he never forgot about God, and every week when he would get his paycheck, he would send his tithes to church by his mother Edith.

The biggest reason that Francis and her daughter had weighed so heavily on his mind all of these years, was that on Saturday, February 4th, 1978, Louis was at work, he was scheduled to get off at 4:30 P.M., but at about 3:50 P.M., he began sweating profusely, right after that he became nauseous, and at 4:02 P.M., he began vomiting like crazy, something that Louis rarely did, he had always told people that he had a cast iron stomach, and could eat just about anything, that still applies until this day, Louis's supervisor noticed how sick he appeared to be, and told him to leave work early and go home and lie down, which Louis did, however by the time he got home and laid down, he was fine, he felt perfectly normal.

About three hours later, around 7:30 P.M., Francis called Louis from the hospital, she told him that she had just had a baby girl, at, would you believe this, 4:02 P.M., that evening, they talked for a while, Louis told her congratulations and that once she went home, he would stop over and see the two of them, she told him that she would be going home that following Monday morning if all went well. Now of the many things in life that Louis pondered in his heart, this may very well have been the greatest, God in his infinite wisdom had set all the wheels in motion for this.

That Monday evening, Louis did go to visit Francis and the new baby just as he had said he would, and immediately he was smitten, he fell hard for this beautiful baby girl, whom Francis had named Maeline, and for Francis as well, the feelings were reciprocated. From that evening on, the three of them were almost inseparable, and for a whole year and a half, this went on, Louis had even told me that he had talked to Francis about the two of them getting married, this was all of course before they had grown a little tired of each other and their relationship finally went sour.

I knew Francis also, if you will recall the kind of woman that I said Edith Timm's was, the Timm's family moved often, and wherever Edith lived, she made a lasting impression on her neighbors with not only her spirituality, but with her virtue and integrity as well. Many of her neighbors would often came to church with her, many of the members that are there, are there because of Edith, and it was when the Timm's family had lived near Francis and her family, that as young girls, Francis and two of her sisters would often come to the church with the Timm's famly.

There was a period of approximately three years, from 1976 until 1979, that the public transportation system, was my main source of transportation. I would often see Francis on the bus as I traveled, and I would question her, and ask her why wouldn't she act right and marry Louis, she was very honest about it, which was one of the reasons that she and Louis were able to be as cordial with each other as they were. Francis told me that she felt she was not good enough for Louis, she said that she had always thought that Louis was special, that he was a morally good man, and that he deserved someone better than her, she just felt that she was not right for him, that honesty has helped them to maintain a lifelong friendship until this very day. Also, I did go back and relay this conversation that she and I had, to Louis.

Now that we've gotten past this explanation of the soul searching that Louis had often been experiencing, there was still something else that had also troubled him deeply, he had always been a very responsible individual, and whereas he had always thought about and wondered if Maeline was his child, by the same token he had also always wondered if Junior was really not his child, and though he often asked, Carol always told Louis that he was the only man that she had ever been intimate with.

By the summer of 1992, Louis had become pretty much fed up with his wife and all of her mystery, as well as with many of the other things that surrounded his life, after much urging, that second summer that he and Carol were in there new home, he finally persuaded Francis, after asking her for ten years, to allow him to take the two of them, her and Maeline, to a lab, so that the three of them could have some DNA tests run, and have this mystery put to rest, once and for all.

Now at home he had told Carol that he only wanted to take Junior with them, just to have him tested with Maeline, to see if he and Maeline's DNA matched each others, the timing in this matter, was all a part of God's big picture in the life of Louis, any sooner or any later, the outcome could have been a fatal one.

Once all the appointments were made, and all of the tests had been ran, the lab told them that the results would be back in approximately four to six weeks. Carol told Louis that she didn't know why he wasting his money, especially having the tests ran on Junior, however Louis said to Carol, I feel that I am following the Lords leading.

Throughout the time that they were waiting for the test results, Louis continued to ask Carol, was there anything that she wanted to come clean and tell him, she continued to maintain her innocence by saying that he was the only one she had ever been intimate with, and there was no doubt in her mind as to who the father of Junior was.

In Louis's heart and mind, he had always wanted to be certain, where Maeline was concerned, he felt that he had a little money now, and that if it turned out that she was his daughter, in the event that anything should ever happen to him, he would like to have provided a little something for her in his will, with the uncertainty that had surrounded everything up until this point, had something happened to him, she would have had nothing coming, again, Louis just wanted to do the right thing, before man and God.

Louis had done certain things for Maeline, he had given her money, bought her things, he even had her over to spend the weekend with he and his family on more occasions than he could count, why you might ask, if there was so much doubt there, because Louis had been there for the whole first year and a half of her life, and on occasion, he would ask Francis, if you continue to insist that Maeline is not my child, why would you allow any man to take your daughter with him for the weekend, Francis assured him that it was not just any man, it was him, and only him, she said to Louis, that I know you, I know the type of person that you are, my daughter does not have a male figure in her life right now, except for you, I have known you since we were about ten years old, and I trust that you will take care of Maeline, just as if she were your very own, you have always been that kind of a person. Again, our God will prepare the way for those whose heart is stayed on him.

On a Tuesday evening, approximately four weeks later, Louis arrived home, the tests results were there, he decided that he would wait until Carol arrived home to open them. After about an hour had passed, Louis, waiting with great anticipation, heard Carol arrive at home, Louis was upstairs in the bedroom, he called out to Carol to come upstairs, which she did, there he sat at the foot of the bed and held up the unopened test results, once again he said to Carol, is there anything that you would like to tell me, this time she said yes there is, and she began to talk, she said that for all of these years that you have continued to ask me if Junior was really your son, it has really disturbed me, a woman knows with whom she has been intimate, and now in my heart I am really glad that you had these tests ran, so that you can finally quit listening to the Devil put these thoughts into your mind about Junior, I know that he is your son, and now beyond the shadow of a doubt, you will now know also.

Louis sat there, slightly embarrassed now for having the tests ran, one mind said that he should apologize to her for doubting her in the first place, after all, how does one genuinely discern the voice of God, how do you truly know when the Lord himself is speaking to you:

2nd Corinthians 11:14-15

"And no marvel; Satan himself is transformed into an angel of light. Therefore it is no great thing if his ministers also be transformed as the ministers of righteousness; whose end shall be according to their works."

Matthew 24:24

"For there shall arise false Christs, and false prophets, and shall show great signs and wonders; insomuch that, if it were possible, they shall deceive the very elect sake."

The more that Louis thought about it, the more he said to himself, I know that I could not have missed the voice of God and be this far off, he thought to himself, how I would love for these results to now reveal that Junior is my biological child, and that Maeline is not, how much it would now simplify things in his mind and in his life. Finally he would be able to get on with his life and with his wife now, having no further reservations about her, you see if Junior had not been his, then his whole marriage was a lie, seeing as though he had only married Carol, because she claimed to be pregnant by him in the first place.

Go ahead, open the results Carol urged him, as she sat there thinking to herself, I'm really going to rub his face in this one, there are many women out there who have gotten themselves into these kinds of predicaments, and really did not know who the father was, or had tests ran only to reveal that the very one they thought was the father, was not, this was not the case here at all Carol thought to herself, he's going to pay for a very long time for doubting me, I'm going to have him wrapped around my little finger, he'll be so sorry and apologetic, that he'll do anything that I ask him to do.

Louis opened the results, never having seen anything like this before, it wasn't as easy to read as he had originally thought, as he sat there looking it over, Carol, not even seeing the results for the way they were sitting, said, now what did I tell you, I knew that Junior was yours all the time, I don't even have to ask you what the results say, now do I, not really Louis said, and he showed her the results, which had showed him what the probability of him being Junior's dad were.

Louis knew many friends and relatives, as I'm sure most people do, who have had these burning questions about the paternity of a child, a great many have never gone through the trouble of finding out the truth, it is a beautiful thing, when a woman can say beyond the shadow of a doubt, that I know who the father of my child is, and this goes for the single and the married women. At one of the larger, more well known hospitals here in this city, they have statistically proven that somewhere between ten and twenty percent, of all the children that are born here, the man that is presumed to be the biological father, is not.

Not only here, but many hospitals have reported that they have many people that come in for bone marrow tests, for blood transfusions, for transplants, only to find that the father, grandfather, son or nephew, is not a genetic match, and many times could not even possibly be related to the person for which they want to be a donor. In these cases the hospitals hands are tied, and legally, this is a can of worms that it would be best if they did not even think about opening, therefore, they can only tell these individuals that they were not a match. I often wonder if these individuals, namely the women realize that they are not only lying to God, but they are shortchanging themselves and their children, and their children's children robbing them of their true ancestry.

Two of the hardest words to say in the English language are "I'm sorry", many would rather die, be cut off from loved ones and God, and miss their eternal blessings, because they simply refuse to come clean. If you are willing to ask for forgiveness, even if the one whom you have offended, refuses to forgive you, God will, and if we truly want to please God, and exemplify the type of character and the qualities that he alone possesses, these two little words must be in our vocabulary, try as we might, there is no getting around it, there are certain things, that we must confess with our own mouths, before the healing process of God can begin in the life of an individual,

1ˢᵗ John 1:9

"If we confess our sins, he is faithful and just to forgive us our sins, and to cleanse us from all unrighteousness."

Now back to Louis, who is still sitting there on the side of the bed with the results still in his hand, what these results have just revealed was that the probability of Louis Timm's being the father Louis Timm's Jr, were a big fat "0", the tests read that he was excluded, beyond the shadow of a doubt, Louis sat there, virtually paralyzed, for over two hours, not being able to move or speak, yet his mind was racing at about a thousand miles an hour, total shock and disbelief, not so much that Junior was not his son, but that an individual, could knowingly do this to another individual, and then to be able to stick to a lie like that, and perpetuate it for nearly thirteen years, he was totally and utterly devastated, just thinking to himself;

CHURCH-FOLK SOME MESSED-UP-FOLK

When Louis could finally speak again, he asked Carol what explanation could she possibly have for what these result revealed, I hope that everyone reading this is sitting down, because the explanation that she gave just goes to show how low some people will stoop, and how far that evil and fallen man will go to cover up their sins;

Proverbs 28:13

"He that covereth his sins shall not prosper: but whoso confesseth and forsaketh them shall have mercy."

The explanation that Carol gave to Louis, was that she worked at a hospital, and that they make mistakes on tests all of the time, and once again she assured him that he was the only man that she had ever been intimate with. Louis was now livid, but by this time, he had also become a master at hiding his emotions, he told Carol that it would be better if they discussed this more the next day. It's true, hospitals do make mistakes, but if you know that there is even a remote chance that the results are correct, don't perpetuate a lie. Told you,

"CHURCH-FOLK SOME MESSED-UP FOLK"

Now the next day, what Louis had in his heart and mind, was that he would call the lab where the tests had been ran, so that he could personally talk to the doctor himself, and he did just that, it was a woman doctor, she was very polite and sympathetic with him, she assured him that the results were totally accurate and that his feelings were totally normal, Louis told her that he would like the tests to be ran again, she told him to please not waste his money, she said that if there was an error on the labs part, that the tests would be free, but if they came back with the same results again, that he would have to pay the seven hundred dollar fee all over again.

What this doctor went on to explain to Louis was, that in her years of doing this she had seen just about everything that there was to see, she said there were women who would bring their children in for tests with numerous men, while their husbands were either at work or out of town on business, men that would bring their children in while their wives were at work or out of town, tests showing that the child may not have been the fathers, but it was someone related to him, one woman even came in and had her child tested with her husbands father, give it some thought she told Louis, sleep on it and call me back tomorrow.

Louis did think about this, he called the doctor back the next day and he told her that even if he would have to pay seven thousand dollars, that he was going to prove beyond a shadow of a doubt, that his wife was a liar, and to make her come clean with him once and for all, the doctor agreed to set up another appointment for the two of them, Louis told her that it would be for two children again, this time he was having Byron tested along with Junior, just to be on the safe side.

After approximately four of the longest, most intense weeks that a person could have waited for, again the results were in, this time, they revealed pretty much what Louis expected them to reveal, again, the tests revealed that Junior was not his biological son, and that Byron was. This time however, Carol was livid, she said that she felt like most men would have taken their wife's word, and left it at that, this time, she did admit to half the truth, she finally, in light of this new evidence, admitted that Louis was not the only man that she had been intimate with, she said that there had been one other man, but she was just so sure that Junior could not have been this man's, which is why she had never owned up to it. Just in case you're wondering, Maeline's test results came back that showing that beyond a shadow of a doubt, she was the biological daughter of Louis.

Louis was sorely displeased, not only with his wife and his life, but also with himself,

Psalm 51:3

"For I acknowledge my transgression: and my sin is ever before me."

Louis partially and rightly so, felt that he had no one to blame for this mess but himself, if he had not been so promiscuous, if he had not committed fornication with Carol in the first place, if she had just told him that there was this possibility that the child wasn't his, if if if, we cannot continue to hypothesize over what could have or what should have happened, it didn't happen that way, you see the way that it has happened, now where does one go from here.

Louis gathered up some of his clothes, and checked into a local hotel for a week. Isn't it just like God, to take us out of our comfort zone, to take us where he wants us to go. Louis had some very deep discussions with God during this time, he had always felt that marriage was till death do us part, he now felt like something had died within him, and that this marriage was also dead.

During this week long stay at the hotel, he would talk to Carol on a daily basis, she assured him that aside from this one discretion, which she reminded him, had taken place before they were even married, she swore that she had never been unfaithful to him during their marriage. After that week, Louis went back home, and after talking to Carol's parents, as well as his own, he decided that he was going to try and make his marriage work, after all he said to himself, the vows that they had taken said for better or worse. If this was what he considered worse, he was in for a very rude awakening.

Louis returned home that following week, but as you may well know, things would never be the same, and he would never look at Carol quite the same way either. It seemed as if now, there was no contentment in his soul, pray as he might, he could not find rest for his spirit, joy and forgiveness were fleeting. There were times that he would look at Carol, and the very sight of her would nauseate him, and this displeasure that he now had with her, he did not try to hide. Carol would often tell Louis that she refused to live under these conditions, to which Louis would always respond, there isn't a thing keeping you here.

Louis did not believe in hiding things, he felt that just as there are sins of commission, there are also sins of omission, therefore when they had first received the test results from the DNA lab, he explained the entire situation to Junior, and on both their parts, the results seem to do little, if anything at all to diminish their relationship, after all neither of them had done anything at all wrong to warrant such deceitfulness.

Louis even tracked down Junior's biological father, he then retained a lawyer, then he sued and forced him to take a paternity test, once the results confirmed that he was the biological father, Louis then sued for child support and arrearages, for Junior. I had always known that Louis was nobodies fool, he had always loved to study, and had taken some law classes after graduating from high school, and with what he was contemplating doing, he knew that certain things had to be in place first, or it could and would cost him dearly, Louis won the child support for Junior, however when it came to getting the arrearages, Carol told them that this would not be necessary, again this incensed Louis, she would need it worse than he would.

What Louis knew, was that two men cannot be ordered by the courts to pay support for the same child, he also knew that under the law, the husband is presumed to be the child's biological father, and that in the event that a divorce should occur, the order of support would be against the husband, and that once this happens, God almost has to come down himself, to have it either lifted or switched, just ask any man that has found himself in this predicament.

After about three months of pure chaos, living in the house with what Louis often considered, an unrepentant woman, of whom he said most of the time, she walked around like nothing had happened, like she had done nothing at all wrong, Louis could no longer take it, he told Carol that something had to change if they really wanted to stay together. He told Carol that it appeared to him that she thought she was doing him a favor by staying there, he assured her that she was not, and that if he had not had the mind that he wanted to please God, this so called relationship that they had would have ended long before it got to this point.

Another problem came to the surface around this same time, Louis got a call from the bank where some of his accounts were held, he was told that a check had been cashed on one of his accounts, it turns out the person who wrote the check did not have enough to cover it in their account, therefore the bank was taking it out of Louis's account, over the next week, he received nine more calls informing him of this same thing, the total amount was almost forty thousand dollars. Louis had also been informed by the bank, that his name was no where involved in any of the transactions, they had all been done by a Carol Timms.

1st Timothy 6:9-10

"But they that will be rich fall into temptation and a snare, and into many foolish and hurtful lusts, which drown men in destruction and perdition. For the love of money is the root of all evil: which while

some coveted after, they have erred from the faith, and pierced them-
selves through with many sorrows."

It took Louis three weeks to retrieve his money from the bank, he had
to take Carol to the police station, have her fill out an affidavit for each
check, saying that she was not the one that had cashed it, have each of
them notarized, send them in to the banks fraud division and wait to see
what the outcome would be, after which time, Louis did finally receive his
money back.

1ˢᵗ Corinthians 7:15

"But if the unbelieving depart, let him depart. A brother or a sister is
not under bondage in such cases: but God hath called us to peace."

After this incident Louis had had enough, he told Carol that she had to
either straighten her act up, or that she would have to get out. Most of you
would not believe how she responded to this, she told Louis that she
would be leaving him within the next thirty days, upon this new revelation, Louis then called his attorney and filed for divorce that following
week. Although Carol said that a divorce was not what she really wanted,
but her actions did not bespeak this, and she did leave their home at the
end of that thirty day period and she moved in with her younger sister.

The boys and Louis had always had an excellent relationship, and they
said that they had no desire to move with their mother, so they stayed
there with Louis.

Matthew 5:32

"But I say unto you, Whosoever shall put away his wife, saving for the
cause of fornication, causeth her to commit adultery: and whosoever
shall marry her that is divorced committeth adultery."

After about a month after Carol moved out, Louis heart was softened,
again by listening to church-folk that knew their situation, mainly some of
his own family members, pointing out to him that the only biblical cause
for divorce is adultery, and in spite of how he might now feel, Carol had

said that she had never been unfaithful to Louis during their marriage, and certain of his family members said that they believed her. So late that February, Louis and the boys went over to Carol's sisters house, where he asked her if she would come back home to live with them, which she did, this was all a part of God's divine plan for right now;

Romans 8:28

"And we know that all things work together for good to them that love God, to them who are the called according to his purpose."

Louis needed to know that he was doing the right thing before God, in contemplating a divorce, bringing Carol back home was all a part of God's plan for Louis right now in confirming what he had been contemplating. Louis did not cancel the divorce proceedings, he simply called the attorney, and had them put on hold. Part of what also helped him to deal with this whole situation, was that the company that he worked for had purchased another company that was out of town, and they sent Louis there to work for them, so for six weeks during these trying times, Louis was out of town helping his company out with this transition.

Unknown to Louis, Carol had always thought that he was a real sucker, and the façade that she had been hiding behind for all of these years, while God waited for her to come clean, was about to blow up in her face, for years she had done many little dirty underhanded things, trying to sabotage Louis throughout his entire life with her, but because of an almighty and awesome God that he served, none of them came to naught, and all I could think about was that if God be for you, he's more than the whole world against you.

Louis called his attorney, he told him that he wanted him to get a court order to have Carol's hospital records released to him, still determined to bring some closure to this matter. Now to help understand this, we must start at the very beginning, we must remember that when we begin to dig, we may uncover some things that we were really not prepared for, and some people will be bold enough to tell you that they will go to their grave, never revealing the truth about certain areas of their lives, some will tell you that if you can't prove it, they will always deny it.

Louis had always known and liked Carol in a platonic sense, however in March of 1980, Carol began to come on to him in a sexual way, being a young man, with raging hormones, Louis did not resist, and he began to know her in the biblical sense. One month later, on April 15th, Carol told Louis that she had gone to a doctors appointment that very morning, and had just found out that she was expecting a child, this was the first time that Louis had ever asked her if he was the father, this was also the first time that she had ever told him that he was the only man that she had ever been intimate with.

Louis always being brought up in the church, the son of a minister, asked Carol what did she think they should do, Carol suggested that they get married, Louis left that very afternoon, went and bought a wedding set, brought it back that same day, proposed to her, and they were married on May 4th 1980, less than three weeks after this whole lie was first conceived.

Upon receiving Carol's hospital records, Louis now sat down with her, and for the first time, the scattered pieces of this very intricate puzzle began to unfold. What those hospital records indicated, was that right there in black and white, on February 8th, Carol had a pregnancy test, and she was told on that day, that the results were positive.

Well one might ask, why couldn't Louis do the math and figure this out, well first of all, Carol had told Louis that her due date was in December, now sometime during the middle of September, she had developed toxemia, and after putting on about sixty pounds, she was admitted into the hospital, where after a barrage of tests, lasting about ten days, they decided to induce her labor and to take the child by a caesarean section delivery, and that they did, so on October 6th, 1980, Junior was born.

Now during this time, hospitals did not allow husbands to stay in the delivery room for this kind of birth. Louis had anxiously waited in the waiting room while all of this occurred. When they were done and finally told him that he could go back in the room with Carol, Louis asked the doctor since the child was early, would he be okay, the doctor, at that time assured Louis that all of this was taken into account which was the reason for so many tests, and that although the child had been born early, he would be just fine. Once Louis went back in to see Carol, she also said that that had been one of her concerns, seeing as though the child had been born two months early.

What those hospital records also showed Louis, was that Junior was not two months early, as Carol had originally said, but that he was two weeks early, the records showed an original due date of October 22nd, and in questioning the doctor, Louis was not specific enough, instead of asking about the health risks involved for the child, he should have asked the doctor exactly how early had the child been born.

Upon looking at these records, Louis now asked Carol if she could explain this, and for the first time, Carol finally admitted that she had known that Louis was not the father from the very beginning, she said why should I continue to argue with what you can now see for yourself written in black and white.

Louis had already decided that he was going to put his all into trying to make this marriage work, how many of you know, and have been there yourselves, that it takes two people to make a marriage work, It doesn't matter how hard one person may try, it just will not suffice. After about four months of trying, Louis still felt like it was pure torture, but he said that he was putting all of his faith in the fact, that the will of God would ultimately be done. When you put your total faith and trust in God, he will not leave you, nor will he forsake you, though the road that you're traveling may get rough, and the pressures of life seem more than you can bear, God can still speak peace in the midst of the storms of life, even as they rage all around you, God will be your peace in the midst of every storm that life may bring your way.

Early that July, they also had a major problem that surfaced at the church, three utility companies had come out to shut the lights, gas and the telephone off, for non-payment of services, that were now over three months in arrears. Louis was one of the board members that served on the church council, therefore he called an emergency meeting that evening with Pastor Evans, the treasurer and the rest of the church council members.

At the meeting he asked the treasurer for an explanation on how this could have happened, she told them all right there at the meeting, that she had once opened a piece of mail to see if it was a bill that needed to be paid, the pastor saw her do this and scolded her, he told her that she was to never open the mail at the church, that whenever there was a bill that needed to be paid, he would give it to her himself and let her know to pay it.

When Pastor Evans was asked for his explanation in this matter, he said that he had only told her that, trying to make sure nothing got misplaced or slipped through the cracks. Louis then said that that was fine, but still why hadn't they been paid, Pastor Evans said that he had simply put them on his desk, then some papers had inadvertently covered them up, and that he had just honestly forgotten about them.

Well Louis said, one month you might forget, two months, there's a problem, three months and you're trying to cover something up. The church council members unanimously agreed that the treasurer was to now open all bills and pay them in a timely fashion, which the Pastor said he was in agreement with.

Louis said that they would now need to go over all of the church finances to see exactly were they stood as a church financially, he asked Pastor Evans for the church checkbook and the bank statements, Pastor Evans said that they were at home in his nightstand, and that he would bring them back the next evening. The council members agreed that this needed their immediate attention, therefore they would all come back the following evening to continue this.

That following evening they all did just that, Louis once again asked Pastor Evans for the checkbook and the bank statements, this time however, Pastor Evans told Louis that he was the pastor, and that after giving it much thought, Louis had no right in demanding that he bring these things in, therefore he was not going to. Louis then called for a church meeting, a meeting that would now consist of the entire congregation, to be held that next Sunday.

Louis explained to the church exactly what had happened, that the members of the church council had asked for the records and that Pastor Evans had refused to bring them in, when Pastor Evans was asked about all of this, he stood there before the entire congregation and began to cry, he said forgive me, for I have misappropriated some of the churches money, it turned out that every penny the church had in the bank was now gone.

Someone in the congregation said, just let it go and lets go on from here and try to make sure that this never happens again, the biggest portion of the church said that they were in agreement with this, so they all decided to put it behind them, Louis never looked at Pastor Evans the same after this, only thinking to himself every Sunday now as he watched Pastor Evans preach, that

"CHURCH-FOLK SOME MESSED-UP-FOLK"

Also late that July, Louis became ill once again, he began running a very high fever, and after three days of battling with what he thought was a summer cold, at Carol's insistence, he broke down and went to the emergency room. Once there, after an hour of tests and blood work, the attending physician sat down to tell him what they had diagnosed, what she told him was that of all of the tests results had now come back, and they showed that he had tested positive for having a sexually transmitted disease, Louis was not only in total shock and disbelief, he said to her that there had to be a major mistake, he told the doctor that he had not been unfaithful to his wife, and that there was no way possible, that these results could be accurate.

What we must realize, is that doctors run into these type of situations all the time, where an individual in what they may think, is a committed and monogamous relationship, is in denial at the time of a crossroad such as this one, and the doctor does not have a vested interest in their relationship, therefore, they may seem to lack the necessary compassion that it takes in breaking this kind of news to someone.

What this doctor told Louis, was that if he knew that it wasn't him, then he also knew who it had to be, she then took out an object that sort of resembled a metal Q-tip, only about twice as long, she then told Louis to drop his pants so that she could get a culture sample, Louis refused, he said you're not going to stick that in me, the doctor was flabbergasted, she said that she had never had anyone refuse before, and that she would have to note this in his chart, that the patient refused to let her test him, Louis told her that she could note anything in there that she wanted to, that he would not subject himself to this, and to just give him a few moments of privacy.

Louis knew exactly what he wanted to do, he went out into the lobby and called Carol, he explained the entire situation to her, and told her to come to the emergency room as quick as possible. Carol did just that, once she arrived, the doctor took her in and tested her for an STD, the tests all came back with a negative reading for any kind of sexually transmitted disease, making Louis look all the more like the bad guy, the doctor noted in her chart that the wife checked out just fine and that Louis had refused to let her treat him. Now these doctors don't know you from Adam, they don't know, or really care who the culprit is in these situations, they are simply there to do their jobs.

Romans 8:37

"Nay, in all these things we are more than conquerors through him that loved us."

Nevertheless the doctor gave them both a prescription for some penicillin, so that the disease would not be passed back and forth between the two of them and sent them on their way. Still this did not sit well with Louis at all, it now looked like maybe he was the one at fault, even though in his heart, he and God knew, if no one else did, that he had no reason to be worried, for he knew what he had done, or in this case, he knew what he had not done, when you know that you have a clear conscience, in any given situation, stand still and see the salvation of the Lord, for it is in him alone that we are more than conquerors, whatever the battle may be.

10

"THE STORM IS PASSING OVER"

1st Corinthians 7:10

"And unto the married I command, yet not I, but the Lord, let not the wife depart from her husband:"

1st Corinthians 7:15

"But if the unbelieving depart, let him depart. A brother or sister is not under bondage in such cases: but God has called us to peace."

Louis was still more than just confident, that something in their marriage was just not right, he simply couldn't prove anything though, and Carol just wasn't willing to talk about it. The only consolation that he had at all, was that God is always on the side of right, and this alone was enough for him.

Louis told Carol that this just wasn't working, that their marriage had had a pretty long run, and that it was time they ended this farce and just put It all behind them. It was at this time that another unexpected first occurred, Carol finally admitted that she was seeing someone else, she also told Louis that this someone, had already told her that he would take care of her, and now she said, that she was in total agreement with Louis concerning their marriage, and that hopefully the transition would be a smooth one, on both their behalves, she also told him that part of her staying this long, was a fear of the unknown, but that now, she knew this other individual could provide for her just as good as Louis had always done.

That last week in July, Carol went out and found an apartment for herself, she paid the first month's rent and security deposit on it, she then came home and showed Louis the receipt that she had been given, and told him that this time she meant business, however, she told him that the apartment leasing agent had said that it would not be ready until September 1st, Louis told her that this would be just fine with him, all the while, grieving on the inside.

Job 18:8

"For he is cast into a net by his own feet, and he walketh upon a snare."

Still believing in his heart that God would possibly work a miracle out in this situation, Louis was now grasping for a shred of anything that could possibly change the outcome of their inevitable plight. Could God really bring them to this point and not work out a miracle in their situation. Now tell me, exactly what point is it that God is bringing one to, we cannot continue to make bad choices, and point the finger at God, it is by our own choices that we are brought down:

James 1:13-15

"Let no man say when he is tempted, I am tempted of God: for God cannot be tempted with evil, neither tempteth he any man: But every man is tempted, when he is drawn away of his own lust, and enticed. Then when lust hath conceived, it bringeth forth sin: and sin, when it is finished, bringeth forth death."

Louis, always one for thinking well ahead, again he called the attorney, and told him to go on full steam ahead with the divorce proceedings, just in case God did not intervene, he felt that he could always stop it again if necessary. What Louis was mostly afraid of, was that if Carol went out into the world, that even with good intentions, she might be unduly influenced by someone to try and take advantage of his kindness.

That following week, Louis, Carol and the boys went on what would be their last vacation together as a family, they went to visit his maternal grandmother and some of his other relatives that lived about a twelve hour drive away. Louis also let all of his relatives know that this would most likely be the last trip that Carol would probably be taking with him, because once they returned home he told them all, that they would most likely be finalizing their divorce. The entire vacation was absolutely beautiful, so much so, that again, Louis prayed to God, that in his infinite wisdom, he would lead him to do the right thing.

Proverbs 16:7

"When a man's ways please the Lord, he maketh even his enemies to be at peace with him."

When it is a man's (or woman's), sincere desire to please God, and to walk according to his statutes and commands, God will prosper him in his journey, we cannot expect to be hokey pokey Christians, and still enjoy the blessings and faithfulness of a faultless God, he knows our hearts, and anyone thinking that they can have a shallow relationship with God, does not know him, in the power of his saving grace:

Daniel 2:22

"He revealeth the deep and secret things: he knoweth what is in the darkness, and the light dwelleth with him."

Louis did not know the evil spirit that Carol was operating in, but God did, we can only look on the surface and see what an individual is doing, but God looks beyond that, to why an individual is doing what he is doing, he sees the ulterior motives at work in all of us,

Hebrews 4:12-13

"For the word of God is quick, and powerful, and sharper than any twoedged sword, piercing even to the dividing asunder of soul and spirit, and of the joints and marrow, and is a discerner of the thoughts and intents of the heart. Neither is there any creature that is not manifest in his sight: but all things are naked and opened unto the eyes of him with whom we have to do."

The end of that August, this whole thing weighed very heavily upon Louis, seeing as though the time was very quickly approaching when Carol was supposed to move out. As that infamous final day approached that would be their last day in that home together, that evening, Louis talked to Carol very good, one last time, to make sure that she knew exactly what it was that she was doing, she assured him that she did.

Louis had to work that following day that Carol had planned on moving out, and he had already told her that he was glad he did, because he refused to have any part in her leaving, she told him that she had already worked things out with her brother and that he would be coming over to help her move, Louis told her to take whatever it was that she wanted, and they would get together the following evening, to wrap up whatever last minute business there was.

That following morning Louis left for work just like he had always done, his soul was very weary and heavy though, but he stuck it out anyway. When he arrived home that evening, her brother had come through for her just as she had said that he would. Louis walked into the house, she had taken the bedroom set, kitchen set, living room furnishings and some of the dishes, the reality of it all finally hit Louis, but if this was what she really wanted, he didn't mind the things that she had taken, all that he could think to himself was, that if she could actually leave him, she had never really been for him to begin with.

She stopped by to drop off his house keys, just as she had promised she would the night before. That first week, she would either stop by or call him each evening, just to see if everything was alright, and although he played hardball, this really did make him feel good.

Everyday when Louis would arrive home from work, Junior and Byron would be there, sitting on his front stairs waiting for him, their feelings now was that they had two homes, Carol also told Louis that he could stop by and visit them anytime, although he said that he really did not want to do that, he did, and occasionally he would, just to ask her if this was what she really wanted, each time she told him that it really was best for the both of them.

Romans 12:3

"For I say, through the grace given unto me, to every man that is among you, not to think of himself more highly than he ought to think; but to think soberly, according has God hath dealt to every man the measure of faith."

Carol did however give Louis an ultimatum of sorts, she told him that if he really wanted their marriage to work, and if he really wanted her to live in the same house with him, that he would have to allow her to come and go as she pleased, as well as allow her to date other men, without questioning it or throwing it up in her face, to which Louis said that he could not, thank God, then Carol told him that she was going to stay out on her own for a year, do her thing, and at the end of that year she would return home to be his wife once again. This clearly is not the thinking of a rational person, but of one that is filled with ones own self.

Galatians 6:3

"For if a man think himself to be something, when he is nothing, he deceiveth himself."

Louis told Carol that she was deluding herself, what gives an individual the right to think that they can toy with another persons emotions like this, without any of us, the world will continue to go on. He told her that this was her last chance, and that once they were divorced, there would be no chance at all for them to ever reconcile, she told him that this was a chance she would just have to take, because she said that she knew that he loved her, and that whatever happened, she knew that he would allow her to come back.

2 Peter 3:9

"The Lord is not slack concerning his promise, as some men count slackness; but is longsuffering to us-ward, not willing that any should perish, but that all should come to repentance."

What Carol was doing, and had been doing all along, she knew it was wrong, but as long as she thought no one else knew, she had continued in this lifestyle, she was not sorry for what she was doing, or had done, she was sorry that she had gotten caught, when an individual is truly sorry, no one has to catch them for them to be sorry, just knowing that God knows will prick them to their heart, many things that God may allow one to do, he allows hoping that the very stench of their sin alone will be enough to convict them, God will only indulge you for so long, then at the appointed time, he himself will pull the cover off of you, there are certain things, that if we would repent of and discontinue, God would cover for us, but when you try to pull the wool over Gods eyes, he will make you an open spectacle for all the world to see.

2 Corinthians 12:2-4

"I knew a man in Christ above fourteen years ago, (whether in the body, I cannot tell; or whether out of the body, I cannot tell: God

knoweth) such an one caught up to the third heaven. And I knew such
a man, (whether in the body, or out of the body, I cannot tell: God
knoweth;) How that he was caught up into paradise, and heard
unspeakable words, which it is not lawful for a man to utter."

Louis may have been at home alone now, but he had a certain amount
of peace about him now, and now God had his time with him, and God
then began to show him some of the great and marvelous things he had
already done for him throughout his life, God began to unfold the mystery
of his godliness to him, through some unique and divine revelations as
only the God and possessor of all infinite wisdom could do.

God began to take Louis back to the days of his early childhood, there
he showed him the many instances where his divine hand of protection
had been over his life, he showed him many things that men meant as evil
to him, but God had turned it around and worked it out for his good, he
showed him the many vast lessons in his life, that only could have been
learned by him, by being brought up in obscure poverty, he also showed
him the many mistakes that he had made, when relying on self, that if he
had just sought out the wisdom and the will of God, could have been
avoided all together, this marriage being one of them.

Most of all God showed him trust, and he let Louis know that from this
point on, just trust me, and all will be well, trust me when you don't hear
me, trust me when you don't feel me, trust me when you don't see me:

Proverbs 3:5-6

"Trust in the Lord with all thine heart: and lean not unto thine own
understanding. In all thy ways acknowledge him, and he shall direct
thy paths."

Mark 11:22

"And Jesus answering saith unto them, have faith in God."

Louis's Faith was being tested as well as strengthened, he was determined, that with the help of God, he would not fold under the pressures

of this life. He loved jewelry, and he often thought to himself, that it takes great pressure and intense heat to create a diamond, and the only difference between a diamond and a worthless piece of glass, is that one was created under pressure and one was not, vastly changing the value of it, with that analogy in mind, Louis was determined that he would be a diamond for God.

He expected storms in life to now come, but he also was expecting the very peace of God sustain him, and to speak peace to him in his times of troubles and testing. He was determined to live for God, and to also have the promises of God in his life, as well as in the lives of those that he came into close contact with.

11

"DIVINE REVELATIONS"

PROVERBS 9:17

"Stolen waters are sweet, and bread eaten in secret are pleasant"

1st Corinthians 14:25

"And thus are the secrets of his heart made manifest; and so falling down on his face he will worship God, and report that God is in you of a truth."

Louis had already made it up in his mind, that once he and Carol were divorced, in light of the problems that had gone on at the church earlier that summer, he had now really lost confidence in Pastor Evans, that he would no longer go to church there. It now seemed to Louis, that when it rains it really does pour.

Louis decided that he would visit a few other churches that he had occasionally passed, which he did, but he could find no peace for his restless soul at any of them, therefore he decided to go back to the church where the rest of his family were at, the church that I had been his spiritual father and mentor at, the church where he had been born and raised at, also the church where he had been dis-fellowshipped at. He really liked the church there where Pastor Evans was, but had resolved within himself, that he would not return to it as long as Pastor Evans was the pastor there.

Louis received the papers from the attorney that second week that Carol was in her new apartment. He called Carol that same evening, to let her know the exact date and time of the hearing, and to see if there had been any change of heart or mind on her behalf, again there was not. The following evening, he even went over and took her and the boys out to dinner, she acted very cold and withdrawn the entire evening.

The following week, on the evening of September 14th, Louis called Carol, he reminded her that the next morning they had a court date to finalize their divorce, and that if she wanted him to, he would be more than happy to pick her up in the morning and take her down to the courthouse with him, she said that she did want him to do that, and he said alright, I'll see you about 8:00 A.M. in the morning. One thing that Louis wanted, was to make sure she was there.

The following morning Louis arrived at Carol's apartment at about 8:00 A.M. just as he had said, she came out, got in the car and assured him that the two of them were doing the right thing. They talked all the way down to the courthouse, small talk mostly, the one thing that she did tell him, was that in these whole thirteen and a half years, you have never really known me.

They arrived at the courthouse at about 8:40 A.M., their hearing was scheduled for 9:00 A.M. They went in and were seated, and they just sat there, watching all of the other cases that went up before them, when their turn finally came, they breezed through it in no time, the local judge asked them a couple of questions, put her stamp on the decree of divorce and certified it, she then told them that they were now divorced. The attorney said that once he had filed it with the courts, he would send them both a certified copy.

After all was said and done, they then left the courthouse, Louis still had to go to work, so he took Carol home, the ride home was not the same, much more somber, Louis was very troubled, thinking that somewhere before it had gotten to this point, that God would somehow throw a monkey wrench into the whole proceeding, but he didn't, Louis was shocked, Carol was stoic, the conversation that they had, all the way home, was non existent. He pulled up to her apartment and dropped her off, and she very politely said thank you and I'll see you later. Louis made it to work by 10:00 P.M.

Does anybody out their realize how hard it must have been, to go through what this young man had gone through, to then have to go to work, not having told anyone about the divorce, and to put in a full days work. But God knew, and this is all that Louis could think about, that entire day, that Lord you know my heart,

Psalm 139:2

"Thou knowest my downsitting and mine uprising, thou understandest my thought afar off."

Psalm 121:1-8

"I will lift up mine eyes unto the hills, from whence cometh my help. My help cometh from the LORD, which made heaven and earth. He will not suffer thy foot to be moved: he that keepeth thee will not slumber. Behold, he that keepeth Israel shall neither slumber nor sleep. The LORD is thy keeper: the LORD is thy shade upon thy right hand. The sun shall not smite thee by day, nor the moon by night. The LORD shall preserve thee from all evil: he shall preserve thy soul. The LORD

shall preserve thy going out and thy coming in from this time forth, and even for evermore."

Once again that evening, God began to speak to Louis in the supernatural, again he took him in the spirit, to certain things that had occurred early in his life, God not only showed him how Carol had been conspiring against him throughout their entire marriage, he also showed him how and that his divine hand of mercy and protection had always sustained him.

Jeremiah 5:26

"For among my people are found wicked men: they lay wait, as he that setteth snares; they set a trap, they catch men."

God showed him that in the church, there are people that are just as corrupt, if not more corrupt than there are out in the world. Some of the things that were revealed to him, were so unbelievable, that the spirit spoke to him and let him know, that if he were to talk to Carol now, she would be willing to own up to a lot of the indiscretions that he had only been suspicious about before, however, no one is going to tell everything.

Louis questioned God, that if this was what he was going to go through, why had God allowed him to marry Carol in the first place. According to the spirit of God, it was not only for Louis own sake, it was so that Carol might see herself also, had Carol not deceived Louis in the very beginning, what he now thought was a mess in his life, would be nothing compared to the way his life would have unfolded had he stayed a single man much longer, we won't even go into what would have happened to Carol and where she would have ended up.

Carol had always been a very submissive wife, she had an excellent spirit, and she was always very tolerable of most of Louis's idiosyncrasies, that might have been a problem for many other women. Her biggest flaw was that the spirit of immorality had always possessed her, however, this did not effect Louis, because he did not know anything about all of this, she hid it from all very well.

Louis was shown some of the various scenarios, on how his life most likely would have turned out had he not married Carol, it was not a pretty picture that he was shown, this, coupled with a few other things, made him a much more forgiving person, however, it still left him a very bitter person. In God's own timing, all of this finally came to fruition, had it come out any earlier, or in a different way, Louis himself, would have made a shipwreck of his life, had it come out any later, he would have been either dead, or dying.

From the age of nineteen to the age of thirty-three, Louis and Carol had been married to one another, most women would have left Louis in their early twenties, where at that time, a man like him would have picked up on another relationship or two, or three, that would have been just as bad, or worse than the first, but Carol had stayed through thick and thin, mostly thin in those early days.

In staying in this marriage as long as they had, it had gotten Louis pass a very crucial time in his life, where a man finally begins to look more for the virtue and the intellect in a woman, than that which is just merely pleasing to the eye, when a man can finally see beyond the shallow exterior that she may possess, to the inner beauty, that lies deep within a woman, when a man can finally see the character and the integrity, that will still be there, long after the outward beauty fades away as a flower, when he can see past that which is just her natural beauty, to that which is her spiritual beauty, when he can finally see beyond all of this, he is no longer concerned with just that which will gratify the flesh only.

At this point Louis still could not see anything good coming out of this whole ordeal, but he believed that God had a blessing with his name written on it, and he was determined to please him, come what may, he had the blessed assurance that God would take care of him, he prayed continually for God's guidance, he knew within his heart that God did not bring him to this point in his life, to now abandon him.

Psalms 46:10

"Be still, and know that I am God: I will be exalted among the heathen, I will be exalted in the earth."

Romans 8:28

"And we know that all things work together for good to them that love God, to them who are the called according to his purpose."

One thing after another, God began to reveal to Louis, so much so, that after a while, he began calling Carol on the telephone questioning her. Just as the spirit of God had revealed to him, now she was more willing to talk to him, than she had ever been before, she wasn't volunteering any information, but any question that Louis now asked her, she would truthfully answer, Louis asked her why was she willing to be so truthful now that they were divorced, she said that's just it, I'm not your wife anymore, therefore, I don't have to hide anything from you anymore, however some of the questions that Louis chose to ask her, she said that there was no way that he could have known these things, unless he had hired a private detective to follow her.

Galatians 1:12

"For I neither received it of man, neither was I taught it, but by the revelation of Jesus Christ."

Ephesians 1:17

"The God of our Lord Jesus Christ, the Father of glory, may give unto you the spirit of wisdom and revelation in the knowledge of him."

Jeremiah 33:6

"Behold, I will bring it health and cure, and I will cure them, and will reveal unto them the abundance of peace and truth."

Luke 12:2

"For there is nothing covered, that shall not be revealed; neither hid, that shall not be known."

Louis went over to visit with Carol the following day, they began to talk about the telephone conversation that they had the night before, the one thing that he assured Carol of, was that he had never spent one dime on private detectives, what he knew, was directly revealed to him by God himself, and that a private detective could probably not have been as thorough and as vivid, as the spirit of God had been in showing him all of these things that had been revealed to him.

Louis asked Carol why, if she had known that she was already pregnant, would she go to such great lengths to deceive him. Carol explained, that this was because she knew him, she knew the type of person that he was, and that she knew he had always believed in doing what was right, whereas the other man, Junior's biological father, was rotten to the core, and she knew this, but it seems as if these types of men have a stronghold on women, they use and abuse them at will, and it seems as if the women keep coming back for more, as if they are doormats, asking to be continually walked on by the man.

Matthew 18:6

"But whoso shall offend one of these little ones which believe in me, it were better for him that a millstone were hanged about his neck, and that he were drowned in the depth of the sea."

This was partially the reason that Carol was able to play church so well, when we have those that we look up to with great admiration, only to find that they are not at all what that they may claim to be, we sometimes unknowingly become like them, misleading others in our lives as well. Be careful about the example that you set, as well as those that you may cause to stumble.

Carol said that she was looking out for who she knew would be able to take care of her and her unborn child, and that she knew that the other man didn't care about her at all, he was only looking out for himself, and his own lusts of the flesh, even in her revealing to him that she was with child, this did little to bring out any show of feelings or compassion on his behalf, so for now lets just call Junior's biological father Earl Wilton.

Carol also owned up to the fact that she had also had an ongoing relationship with the gentleman in question and his family, it seems that just about everyone knew about this except Louis and his family. Carol also told Louis that she had often taken Junior over to visit with Earl Wilton and his parents, only telling Junior that they were friends of the family. She also said that she had always given them photographs of Junior, whenever they would have any taken.

Now all of this in and of itself is not so bad, but this Earl Wilton that we keep referring to just happens to be the pastor of a church, and his mother is a church mother and secretary, and I use great caution in protecting the identity and not elaborating too much, just in case there is a second book to go along with this one titled

"PREACHERS ARE MESSED-UP-TOO"

Just a little something to think about, so for now, let's just keep calling him Earl Wilton, others things just may surface.

Louis now began to ask Carol about some of the things that had troubled him in the past, being revealed to him only in the spirit. Now earlier when we talked about the break in at the neighbor, Mr. Smith's house, Carol told him that it had been Minister Earl Wilton, Junior's biological father and two of his friends, she said that they had been having an ongoing affair, and that she had never told him to do this, but that she had planted the seed, she said that what she told him, was that if she were to leave Louis for him, it would really be a struggle financially, and that she seriously doubted that she could get, or even afford the house, but if something were to happen to Louis she told Minister Wilton, it would all be paid for free and clear, in addition to this she would also receive a monthly Social Security check for both of the boys, from that point on she said, Minister Wilton took it upon himself, to handle it from that point on.

Now this is how he had planned it all, he and his two friends would come over and break in their house, they would then go in and shoot Louis, after they made sure that he was dead, Minister Wilton would then have sex with Carol while his two friends made sure that the boys stayed in their bedroom, they would then leave the house, Carol would then call the police, report that someone had broken into the house, raped her, and killed her husband, and the only part that she had to play in all of this, was to get up sometime during the middle of the night and turn the alarm off, so that it would not go off once they had broken in, which if you will remember, she had played her part well, I told you

"CHURCH-FOLK SOME MESSED-UP-FOLK"

Why then you might ask, didn't they just go next door when they first found out that they had broken into the wrong house, Carol told Louis, what Minister Wilton had told her, that this would have been to easy for the authorities to figure out, that this whole thing had been a set up all along, if they had done all of this in the same night.

Louis then asked her about that night that he had been too sick to go to work, when the neighbor boy had seen someone outside their garage, this Carol explained to him, that since the first attempt had not worked out as they had originally planned, Minister Wilton had already robbed someone on the next street the week before, and shot him in the process, in doing that, if he then robbed and killed Louis, the authorities would have just thought that it was someone robbing people at random in their neighborhood, again, God's divine intervention had taken place.

Carol told Louis that she had seen God's hand in operation throughout his life, and that she had hated the way that it had seemed God had always worked on his behalf, the many times that others would have cracked under the pressures that he had in life, yet it had always seemed that he came out smelling like a rose. Carol told Louis of the many times she had wished bad luck and misfortune upon him, and how she had always seen how God had given him his unmerited favor, she told Louis that at times she almost hated him, just for that reason alone. Is it any reason for people to hate you just because God blesses you, take heed, for these things they will do.

Psalm 23:4

"Yea, though I walk through the valley of the shadow of death, I will fear no evil: for thou art with me; thy rod and thy staff they comfort me."

Louis continued to ask her about certain occurrences that had gone on throughout their marriage, she continued to answer his questions, some of the questions that Louis asked her were so complex, that this was what had made her believe that he had hired a private detective to follow her, again Louis assured her, that everything he knew, God alone had shown it to him, not only had no one told him, most people, he told her probably would not have even believed most of these things, if she had not owned up to the part she played in most of them herself.

Jeremiah 23:24

"Can any hide himself in secret places that I shall not see him? Saith the Lord. Do not I fill heaven and earth? Saith the Lord."

Louis asked her about the time that he had gotten sick, when the doctor told him that he wanted to do some sort of exploratory surgery in his head, this she explained to Louis, came about when another gentleman, whom we'll just call Ronald Rogers for now, whom she had also been having an ongoing affair with, gave her some kind of drug to began putting into Louis's food, this particular gentleman was a sales representative for a pharmaceutical company, that she had met, through working in the pharmacy. When Louis had first began to go and have these various tests run, Ronald Rogers told Carol to stop with the drugs, because if they ever found them in his system, they would know that this was not just something that anybody had access to, and this could be trouble for he and Carol both.

Louis went on to ask Carol about that morning that she had gone to visit her mother, and on the way home the transmission went out on the automobile. Again she was honest and told Louis that she had not gone to visit her mother, she had been downtown to a hotel with a man that we'll just call for now Clarence Bowers, once she had the problem with the car, that's when she called her mother, and the two of them concocted this story, saying that she had been over that morning visiting with her mother.

This in and of itself, brought out another divine revelation, you see at one time Carol had what Louis thought were the perfect working hours, 9:00 A.M. to 1:00 P.M., well even though Carol brought home a note from her supervisor showing a change of her hours, it was not the supervisors idea at all to change Carol's hours, it was Carol that had requested this herself. It turned out that she had a couple of clients that could only be seen at 9:00 A.M. in the morning.

There were certain men, that when they wanted to contact Carol, it was her mothers number that they would normally call, in turn, Carol's mother would then call Carol, and tell her, that when the opportunity presented itself, Carol was to call her back, so that the two of them could talk when Louis was not around, all of this had gone on for quite sometime, unknown to Louis.

Jeremiah 17:9

"The heart is deceitful above all thing, and desperately wicked, who can know it."

Louis also asked her about the time that he had to go to the emergency room, when he had gotten sick and was told that he had tested positive for a sexually transmitted disease, Louis wanted to know how it was that she came in, and her test came back negative, when he knew that he had not been unfaithful, this she reminded him, that since she worked in the pharmacy, once she found out she had it, she had already taken the necessary medication she needed and cleared her problem up, but naturally she couldn't tell her husband about this, now could she.

There were so many things that Louis had questions about, the fact that she was now answering them, gave him some closure, but the anger and bitterness only grew within him. As he continued to talk to Carol, he knew that if he wanted her continued co-operation, that he would have to maintain his composure, which he did, while a fire burned deep down inside, he once told someone that he could have choked her to death with his bare hands and felt no remorse about it.

Louis asked her about the night that he had arrived home from work, and there was a naked man out near the street and he called the police, this she told Louis, was Minister Earl Wilton, the two of them had fallen asleep while in bed, and Carol said that she knew that he normally arrived home at about 12:45 A.M., she said when the two of them awakened, the clock on the nightstand read 12:45 A.M., and if he had taken even one minute to put his clothes on, she told him that Louis would have probably caught him walking out of the door as he pulled into the driveway.

There was however one area that Carol was not nearly as co-operative in discussing with Louis, this was when he would ask her anything about Bishop Gray, he specifically asked her about the time Bishop Gray had come into town and called, asking Louis to come up to his hotel room to meet with him, the time that he had asked him about the fifteen thousand dollars, Louis had for a long time suspected that Carol had been having an affair with Bishop Gray, and he had asked her about it on more then one occasion, this is where Carol said she drew the line and could not talk about this, she said that even if this were true, she would never have it said that she was the cause, or played any part in the downfall of this man's ministry.

It is silly women like this, that Pastors like Bishop Gray will prey on, and they will continue to do it as long as there are those women out there, that will allow them to do it, no woman is the cause of a man's ministry going down, if he allows himself to get into these ungodly predicaments, he is the cause of his own ministries downfall, these type of men have learned how to manipulate women though, putting them on a guilt trip by making them think like this. There are also many ministers out there, that will tell these type of young women, that it is a part of their service to God, to have relations with them, they can't fool all of the women in the church, but trust me, they usually know the ones that they can fool.

2nd Timothy 3:6

"For of this sort are they which creep into houses, and lead captive silly women laden with sins, led away with divers lusts"

Louis asked her, what about that day she had not gone to work, and had come home late that evening with her parents, now this answer disturbed Louis more than all the other truths that she had given him thus far, because originally she had lied about this. What she now told him though, was that day, as she said she had done several times before, she had gone to the airport, jumped on a plane, went out of state for a liaison with a gentleman there that she knew, only this time, she missed the 4:00 P.M. return flight home, that she had normally taken, and had to take the 7:00 P.M. flight, this scarred her, and she told Louis that she was really afraid that he might suspect something that night.

On the inside Louis was crying like a baby, but he would not let Carol see him cry, he told her that he had to get home, and that he would talk to her later in the week. That night Louis went home and it seemed as if his whole world had come to an abrupt end, all he could think of, was how could she, where would she, why would she, why would God allow her to do such things, he cried like a baby that night, this was the first night that he had been able to cry since Carol and the boys had first moved out. It is in these times, when we are at a spiritual low in our life, that the devil really begins to make you doubt and question God, rest assured that God knows, and he cares about his own.

For two weeks straight, Louis was functioning in what appeared to be an almost coma like state, he would go to work, come home and shut himself off from the rest of the world. Each night he would cry himself a river of tears, ending up with a terrible headache. He would then get on his knees and fervently pray each night, pleading with the Lord, to please take him in his sleep and to not let him wake up the following morning, he sought death with every fiber of his being. I had always preached that there was no forgiveness for suicide, thank God I had, because not only had suicide weighed very heavily on his mind, but so had my words about suicide, I was still in his thoughts.

Psalm 37:1-3

"Fret not thyself because of evildoers, neither be thou envious against the workers of iniquity. For they shall soon be cut down like the grass, and wither as the green herb. Trust in the Lord, and do good; so shalt thou dwell in the land, and verily thou shalt be fed."

Louis was devastated, he felt that his entire life was now over, how could he ever go on he thought to himself, where was his God now he thought, how could this go on for so long, and not one person that he was close to saw any of this coming, if he could shut all of his doors, and never leave the house again, this would be just fine with him. He could never be this cruel to another individual, yet for someone to be able to do this, and it had seemed to not faze them in the least, is a sign that there is a serious underlying problem. Do women have any idea that they are jeopardizing the lives of their entire families. In this day and age, there are too many lunatics around, to put yourself in harms way, by straying from that which God has ordained.

"And it came to pass."

Louis thought about these five little words that so many bible verses begin with, and it came to pass, well it didn't feel like it came to pass, it felt like it came to stay. As these times of trouble appear in our lives, we must have patience, we must remember that God may be trying to tell us something, or to do something in our lives, wait I say on the Lord.

Louis had told his parents that he was now going to put the house up for sale, and from there on out he would play it by ear. His mother Edith, always one thinking with a sober mind, had told him not do anything to hastily, wait on God she said, you always want to be sure that you are doing the will of God, pray without ceasing she told him. Louis promised his mother that he would hold off with things for right now, give it some time, and decide later on down the road exactly what course of action he would take. Louis had never liked living alone, and had prayed much about this, and the very God of peace came in and comforted him, he was never afraid for one moment, in all of the time that he lived there by himself.

Children are usually very resilient in situations such as this, on the exterior they normally seem to adapt very well, in many of these cases, it is often times, many years before some of the problems associated with divorce, or the break-up of what they thought was a very stable home life, may exhibit themselves. For this reason Louis tried to make sure that he was always there for them, and he tolerated a little more of their foolishness than he had normally tolerated from them when they lived there in the house with him, this made the transition for the boys a very smooth one.

12

"DIVINE DELIVERANCE"

PSALM 37:4-5

"Delight thyself also in the Lord: and he shall give thee the desires of thine heart. Commit thy way unto the Lord: trust also in him; and he shall bring it to pass."

PSALM 73:1-3

"Truly God is good to Israel, even to such as are of a clean heart. But as for me, my feet were almost gone; my steps had well nigh slipped. For I was envious at the foolish, when I saw the prosperity of the wicked."

PROVERBS 13:12

"Hope deferred maketh the heart sick: but when the desire cometh, it is a tree of life."

After now being at home alone, and having a two week pity party for himself, Louis began to finally feel and function a little better than he had in the past. He now looked at work as something to help and keep his mind occupied, and home as his place of solitude and rest. He went through and cleaned the entire house, by the time he was done it was almost spotless, you could almost eat off the floor, if he dropped something, he did eat it off the floor. On the exterior he now seemed like he had it all pretty much together.

On the evening of October 1st, Louis's doorbell rang, he went and opened the door and there stood an angel looking at him, it was Tina, she said that her mom had just talked to someone and heard that he was divorced, she then called and told Tina, and Tina said she immediately came over to visit him. Tina told Louis that she had been waiting almost fourteen years for someone to tell her that he and Carol were no longer together.

Now Tina, if you will recall from earlier in the story, was the one that had gotten married, and Byron had served as the ring bearer in her wedding. That same Tina, that when she needed an extra groomsman, Louis had asked her why hadn't she asked him to stand in. Well I said that I would tell you about this later, well now is later, Tina told Louis that there was no way that she was going to stand up there and marry a man, while Louis stood by him as one of the groomsman, because all she would have been doing, was looking at Louis and saying to herself that he was the one that she should really be standing there marrying, she told Louis that she had always loved him.

That evening they talked for a very long time, you see one of the things that I have deliberately omitted up until this time, is that Louis and Tina had dated one another as teenagers, he was the first young man that she had ever been allowed to date. However, the two of them were very stubborn, bull-headed, hard-hearted individuals, who refused to compromise, therefore most of the time their relationship was a very rocky one, yet it was a relationship that went on, right up until the time that he married Carol.

Tina told Louis that he had never known how torn up she was over him, when she found out that he had gotten married, she said that she cried like a baby. She told Louis that this was all behind them now, and that from this point on, it would be just the two of them, she left his home around midnight and told him that she would be back over to see him the next day.

Tina did return the next day, she had also stopped and picked Louis a dinner up, she told Louis that she was determined that this time things were going to work out for the two of them, they were both older and more mature. From this day forward, Tina would come over and visit with Louis every evening after she got off work, this really helped with the overwhelming feelings of anger and bitterness he had been harboring, they had now began to subside. Tina was probably the only woman in the world, that could have gotten this close to Louis at this pivotal time in his life.

Something else that Louis had also wanted to do for a very long time, was to go back to school, Louis now took this opportunity to do that. He enrolled in one of the local universities, paid the tuition and began attending classes that fall, although this wasn't something he felt he had to do, it gave him a certain amount of personal satisfaction, in addition to this he loved his job and was not looking for a job change at this time.

Although Louis felt that God had always been there for and with him, physically, emotionally and financially, he had still always for some reason felt shortchanged when it came to personal relationships. I believe that this is something many people struggle with, especially our young people, how many of us really feel a commitment from others that even remotely resembles the commitment that we feel to others, especially when we have put our word out there, or someone is truly counting on us to come through for them, we will move heaven and earth to try and do our part, whereas on the other hand, what we get is a lackadaisical effort, if any at all, from others to fulfill their commitments, we continually get the short end of the stick, or the raw deal so to speak, and this applies to those in the church and to those that are in the world.

As a relationship between Tina and Louis began forming, it was quite evident that he had his guard up, and rightly so, he had said that the pain of divorce is something that he would not wish on anyone, and he certainly did not want to go through it again. He and Tina were old friends, and he did not want to ruin this, he had even told her that the quickest way that he felt you could ruin a friendship, was to get married.

Louis wanted to take things very slow, she on the other hand, told him that she wanted to marry him, and that if she had her way she would do it today, Louis told Tina that there was no way that he was going to get divorced and marry again all in the same year.

Based solely on that one comment that Louis made, Tina, in her mind began to think, we'll just set a wedding date for January 1st, of the following year, now not only was this in her mind, but in talking to someone else, she had even made the mistake of saying this to that person. Perception is a very dangerous thing, many things have been either created or destroyed based solely on perception, we must always make sure that we have a clear understanding when communicating with others, on either what they perceive, or what we perceive to be the truth.

Divorce to Louis, he felt was worse than death, at least with death it was not by choice, you did not have to see this person that you had once stood before God and man, and said that this was until death do us part, end up with someone else. In death you did not have to hear about what was going on in the life of the one, that at one time had been your significant other, from friends that may still come into contact with them, you never had to worry about being out, and running into one another, you never had to fear receiving that telephone call, saying I'm sorry I left you, I now see the error of my way, can I come back home and we pretend this all never happened.

Life is real, it is not pretend, we've all watched far too many of these fairy tales, with the, and they lived happily ever after endings, unfortunately most of our lives do not end up with the happily ever after endings, they end up with the miserable, wretched, dark endings. We must, as mature individuals, know that some of the situations that we can, and will face in life, must be dealt with, you can not always just turn and run, looking for the easy way out, there is no easy way out.

Even though Louis's confidence level in many of the so called Christians that he knew was now at ground zero, he did still have those that he still revered. It was while talking with one of these individuals, that it came out, that someone was spreading the word that he was getting married on January 1st, this individual told Louis that whatever he did, the Lord had shown them that he was not to get married then, that he was to wait at least one month before getting married.

Louis then went and confronted Tina about these allegations that he had heard about them supposedly getting married on January 1st, it was then that Tina reminded him of what he had said about not getting divorced and then marrying again in the same year, and that she had just assumed that he meant that they could get married anytime in the new year, Louis then reminded Tina that he had never even asked her to marry him yet, Tina then asked him if he would marry her, he said that he would, but based on the conversation he had with that devout Christian, Louis told her that he would not marry her until February 1st, she was disappointed, however she agreed that this would be an acceptable for her.

Once Louis agreed that he would marry Tina, he didn't mind so much her telling people about it, he also began to tell a few others about it himself. Louis even ran into Carol at a store once, he told her that before she heard it from anyone else, that he wanted to tell her that he and Tina would soon be getting married, Carol laughed and told Louis that he wasn't going to marry Tina, She reminded Louis that she had just gone out there to sow her wild oats and that she would be coming back home after a year, once again Louis repeated what he had said, and told her I'm just telling you before you hear it from someone else, he then turned and walked away, leaving Carol standing there wondering to herself, would he really do such a thing to me. Once again I need to be reminded of exactly what it is, that he's doing to her.

That Christmas, Louis gave Carol a large sum of money and told her that it was so that she and the boys would have a memorable Christmas, he had heard that she was hitting it pretty tough financially. What Louis really thought within himself, was that once he married Tina, it would not be the wisest or the most appropriate thing to do, give another woman money, it wouldn't matter what kind of tight she was in. Carol had never had to worry about money, or bills of any sort, she was now getting into an area that was very new to her, where she would find it was not as easy as she may have originally thought that it would be.

For close to five months, Louis lived alone in that big house, the children would sometimes come over on the weekend to spend them with him, in addition to this, just about everyday, Tina would stop by and visit with him for a little while. He cherished those times that he had alone though, and rightly so, for after this brief period, he would not know a time like this, ever again.

One month after the new year rolled in, Louis and Tina were married, just as he had said. Tina told Louis that she really wanted a large wedding and reception, however, Louis told Tina that for second marriages, his personal belief was that this would not be all that appropriate. Note that he said, his personal belief, he did not say that it was wrong, so please don't misquote him, that decision he feels, is an individual preference.

After the normal Sunday morning services were held, Louis and Tina went into Elder Logan's office with a few of their family members, and were married there. Byron was there to take still photographs, and Junior used the video camera to tape the whole thing. After the wedding, Louis and Tina went to dinner, and there Louis gave Tina a key to his house.

Tina and her mother were also members there when I had first arrived to pastor the church in 1964, they had always been very nice, but very private people, that had never been a problem to me, or to anyone else in the church, they were also very faithful members.

One of the things that Louis had been a stickler on, was that he was determined that he was going to set a good example for his children, therefore he had never allowed Tina to spend one single night at his home, he said that when the children got older, that they would never have it to throw up in his face that he had let a woman spend the night with him, that wasn't his wife.

Even his own sisters accused him of allowing Tina to spend the night at his home, what Louis told them, was that he didn't have to prove anything to anyone, God knows, and since Tina lived with her mother, He told them they could ask her mother, she knew that Tina had never spent a single night away from home.

When Junior and Byron went home and told their mother that Louis had gotten married, there was trouble in paradise, Carol went into her bedroom and cried like a baby, she then called and told one of Louis's sisters that she could not believe that he had done this to her, Louis of course was puzzled, and told his sister to please remind me once again, just exactly what it was that he had done to Carol, didn't I tell you

"CHURCH-FOLK SOME MESSED-UP FOLK"

That first year that Louis and Tina were together, it was absolutely beautiful, the two of them seemed to have been soul mates. Louis would often tell her, that he believed it was meant for the two of them to be together all along, which it was, but if they had gotten married when they were younger, it would have never worked out, sometimes God has to take you through a few things, before you can really appreciate him or what he may have blessed you with. Ms. Booker, Tina's mother, would often tell Louis that Tina had always confided in her, that she had always loved Louis, even when he was married to Carol.

Louis's job had recently split into two different companies, Louis was promoted and moved across the street to the smaller of the two companies, this made for a much more intimate setting, Louis's job now also entailed a much greater responsibility, and more people relied on him, to be able to properly do their own jobs.

Tina and Carol looked so much alike, and they were so close in size to one another, that many friends and family members would often tell Louis that he had gone out and tried to find someone as close to Carol as he possibly could, Louis response to this was always the same, he would tell them that he didn't find Tina, she had come looking for him.

Junior and Byron always found it quite amusing that most of Louis's friends and relatives called Tina by Carol's name, although they would always apologize, because some people find being called by their spouses ex-spouses name quite offensive, not Tina, she would tell them, I'm his wife now, and I don't care what name anyone calls me by, it doesn't bother me one bit, and thank God, it really didn't bother her.

Tina had never had any children, and once she had passed the age of thirty, she told Louis that she had pretty much resolved within herself, that she would probably never have any, but now that she had married Louis, she did confide in him that she would like to have a child, while her biological clock was still ticking. Louis told Tina that this was something, that to him, did not make a difference one way or the other, seeing as though he already had three children.

The more that Tina talked about it though, the more that Louis could really see that this was something that she had always desired with all of her heart. One and a half years after the two of them were married, Louis and Tina had a fine baby boy, they named him Eljay.

Louis, if you will remember, came from an extremely large family, Tina on the other hand, came from a family so small, that you could count them all on one hand. Eljay was born with a host of relatives, that he will probably never know all of their names. His birth was almost like that of royalty to Tina and her mother, Tina was Ms. Booker's only child, this made Eljay, her first and only grandchild.

13

"DIVINE JUDGMENT"

Galatians 6:7

"Be not deceived; God is not mocked: for whatsoever a man soweth, that shall he also reap."

2nd Peter 3:9

"The Lord is not slack concerning his promise, as some men count slackness; but is longsuffering to us-ward, not willing that any should perish, but that all should come to repentance."

Numbers 23:19

"God is not a man, that he should lie; neither the son of man, that he should repent: hath he said, and shall he not do it? or hath he spoken, and shall he not make it good?"

We as a people must realize, that God is God, and God will always be God. This is a fact, that try as we may, we can not get around this, God at his most foolish point, outshines us at our wisest point. Man in his finiteness, simply can not comprehend the depth of God's wisdom, when and because he allows us to get by with something, we must not deceive ourselves into thinking that we are getting away with anything. Just as he was patient with Lucifer, he is merely letting us see that the end result of sin will be our eternal damnation, we must awake out of our sleep.

Carol on the other hand, did not fair quite as well, now that she was out on her own, she had to fend totally for herself, not wanting to come off as a pushover, a few months after moving in, she had let her mouth get her into some major trouble at the apartment complex, and she had to hastily move out, not having anywhere else to go, one of her sisters allowed her and the boys to move into her basement, this particular sister had a husband and four children of her own.

Jeremiah 17:5

"Thus saith the Lord; Cursed be the man that trusteth in man, and maketh flesh his arm, and whose heart departeth from the Lord;"

Well, you might ask, what became of the men that she was involved with while she was married to Louis, they all quit speaking to her after her divorce from Louis was finalized. As a man, telling a woman what they want to hear, almost comes naturally, when the woman begins to believe everything that a man tells her, that's the beginning of her problems, she begins to belittle her husband, if not openly, within the confines of her own mind, or within these illicit relationships, she will begin to down talk her husband to the other man, not realizing that this makes her look bad also.

Some men out there prefer a married woman, this involves less ties for them, especially when the man himself is married, when the woman is single, this involves another whole set of problems that some men will tell you that they simply do not want to deal with, and some men, yes even in the church, will tell you that this is why they will only date a married woman.

Carol also began two relationships at this time, with two other married ministers, a Minister James Williams and Minister Gregory Riley, however she favored Minister Williams over Minister Riley, however, like most men that allow themselves to get into these type predicaments, Ministers Williams continued to buy time, by telling Carol that he was getting some business matters straight, and to just give him a little time, which she did, she gave him two whole years, in which he and his wife, in these two years had children numbers four and five. Talk about messed up church folks. Need I say anymore on the matter about

"CHURCH-FOLK SOME MESSED-UP FOLK"

After growing tired of all the lies, and a little wiser, Carol broke it off with Minister Williams, only to get into a full steam ahead relationship with Minister Riley, who was willing to leave his wife for Carol. Carol had began to see what it was like for a woman, to be out there on her own, with little money or experience, when it came to dealing with some of these same men as a single woman. As a married woman, this had not been a problem, she had all of her needs met by a faithful husband at home, whom she at one time had told Louis herself, that she knew that he was faithful to her.

Many women have a price that they can be bought for, many men do also, but the stigma attached is a little different when it's a woman. When times get tough, there are many women that stoop to immoral means for the love of money and materialism, even women in the church who claim to be in right standing with God, often compromise their values, when and if they had just patiently waited for God, he would have brought them divine deliverance. Contrary to what someone might tell you, there are still Jezebel's in the church.

Minister Riley moved Carol from her sisters basement, to an apartment, this would now give him time to straighten out his affairs. Carol also continued to see Minister Williams unbeknownst to Minister Riley. Many men will throw money around like its no big deal trying to impress a woman, it's sad to say, but with many women, this does just that, some-times all the money that a man has is what's right there in his pocket, there are times, that it may not even be his own money that he is impressing the woman with, it may be another woman's.

Once he had done what he considered setting his affairs in order, Min-ister Riley did leave his wife and file for a divorce. When this was all said and done, Minister Riley and Carol were actually married, he later admit-ted that this was the biggest mistake he had ever made before in his life. She had painted herself as the martyr in her marriage to Louis, telling everyone that he was an overbearing tyrant, now that she was married to Minister Riley, he began to see that perhaps she was not being totally true in her portrayal of Louis, he even asked her once, if he's really that bad, why does his new wife continue to stay with him, Carol never did answer that question.

Minister Riley found out about the numerous affairs that Carol had been having while she was married to him, but out of love, he gave it his all trying to make the marriage work between the two of them, but it was all to no avail, she had a demon that was just out of control, finally he told her that he could no longer take it and he too filed for a divorce, and now once again, Carol found herself with nowhere to go. She then asked her younger sister if she and the boys could move in with her for while, and they did.

After a year, Carol's sister had grown very tired of the barrage of men that Carol had constantly coming in and out of her home, also she had not been in the home that long herself, and she felt that she just had no privacy of her own, therefore after a year, she told Carol that she needed to find someplace else to live. Carol found an apartment and moved out, this also strained their relationship. It wasn't long before Carol was engaged again, you guessed it, he had just graduated from seminary when they got mar-ried.

Leviticus 19:36

"Just balances, just weights, a just ephah, and a just hin, shall ye have: I am the Lord your God, which brought you out of the land of Egypt."

Revelation 6:5

"And when he had opened the third seal, I heard the third beast say, come and see. And I beheld, and lo a black horse; and he that sat on him had a pair of balances in his hand."

God always has a way of evening the score, you know how he can balance out a situation like no one else can. One plus God is always a majority, but we must know that in our heart of hearts that we are pleasing in his sight, he knows when we are serving him halfheartedly, and in the moral fiber of our being, we know it also, this is why many times we can't get a prayer through, why our lives seem so empty, it is a dangerous thing to fall out of favor with the living God.

Lamentations 3:44

"Thou hast covered thyself with a cloud, that our prayer should not pass through."

Just like there are Jezebels out in the world, there are also Jezebels in the church, Carol continued to have misfortune follow her, yet she continued to play the martyr. Some of us need not wonder why we can't seem to get a prayer through, we simply need to examine ourselves. As the children grew older, Louis was able to avoid seeing or hearing from, or about her more and more, till finally all contact between the two of them was severed completely.

Louis began to run into people that knew the two of them when they were husband and wife, that were never willing to talk about certain things while he and Carol were married. This one individual even told him that before Carol married him, she was a card carrying prostitute, who had gone in on a regular basis for check-ups at the local clinics for sexually transmitted diseases, whereas many people that Louis now talked to, were now able to attest to this as being factual.

Some of the things that were now told to Louis, he found hard to believe, but in light of what he knew, he now said that he couldn't put anything pass anyone, and from this point on, he purposed in his heart that he would never say what anyone wouldn't do, nor would he let what anyone did do surprise him, ever again.

Matthew 5:44-45

"But I say unto you, Love your enemies, bless them that curse you, do good to them that hate you, and pray for them which despitefully use you, and persecute you; That ye may be the children of your Father which is in heaven: for he maketh his sun to shine on the evil and on the good, and sendeth rain on the just and on the unjust."

You don't just fall out of love, just as falling in love is a gradual process, so is falling out of love, Louis did not hate Carol as some suspected, in light of all that had gone on, he just knew that he no longer wanted their two lives to be any longer entwined, he constantly prayed for her, that the Lord would save her from his wrath to come. Many times he would run into individuals that would say that they had heard of some misfortune that had befallen Carol, his comments often made them think that he did not like nor care for Carol, this was not the case at all, he told one individual that he did not want to see anything bad happen to Carol, but he knew God, and he knew the word of God.

What he knew was, that as sure as the Sun rises in the East and sets in the West, that God is going to pay every man according to his works.

Louis broke off all ties with Carol's entire family. Most of our families are aware of what, and when, if we are doing something that we really have no business doing, but they continually cover for us, not realizing that this only helps us to perpetuate a situation, we must stop sin at the door, look it straight in its ugly face and say to it, you have no authority here, by the power of Jesus name we must rebuke the devourer at all cost, our very soul depends on it, make no truce with the devil, the reward is not worth it.

I recall a time, when Louis's doorbell rang, it was a young man from down at the end of their street, he was looking for Junior, Junior saw him as he approached the house, he told Louis to tell the young man that he wasn't home, as he heard Louis telling the young man to come in, Junior ran into the bedroom and crawled under the bed, Louis kindly escorted the young man into Junior's bedroom, he got down on his hands and knees, and he pointed under the bed and told the young man, there he is, Junior later told Louis that incident was one of the most embarrassing times that he could remember. But you know what, Junior never asked Louis to lie for him again.

1st John 2:16-17

"For all that is in the world, the lust of the flesh, and the lust of the eyes, and the pride of life, is not of the Father, but is of the world. And the world passeth away, and the lust thereof: but he that doeth the will of God abideth forever."

We as a people have become our own worst enemies, we have set ourselves up for one disaster after another, by setting goals for ourselves that are almost impossible to achieve, and at what cost, at the cost of our physical, emotional, psychological and spiritual well being. We must not spend all of our time and effort trying to please, or impress people, what we must desire is a clear conscience, and it is God, and God alone that we must strive to please, and this with our whole being, we simply cannot impress him, what God truly desires of each and every one of us, is a broken spirit, and a broken and contrite heart.

Ecclesiastes 1:2

"Vanity of vanities, saith the Preacher, vanity of vanities; all is vanity."

We must not sacrifice our souls, in our quest for life, we must keep our lives as open books before the Lord, can anyone hide from him, he is holy and just, his glory covers the whole earth.

That year Louis received his Bachelor of Business Administration degree, majoring in Economics, again he was doing all of this for his own personal satisfaction. In addition to this, many of the people that Louis came into contact with, were themselves, highly educated and or very wealthy, therefore they themselves advocated education, a couple of them had even told Louis that in this day and age, he should get as much education as he possibly could.

Louis also found out, in the fall of that year, that Roe, one of the local millionaires that he had befriended years earlier, had passed away, he attended the services, where he ran into a few other wealthy gentlemen that Roe had introduced him to, they told Louis to stop by and see them sometime, he never did.

When Louis had originally met Roe, he had no idea who he was, he didn't really care, then one day, as he, Carol and the boys were sitting in Roe's living room watching television with him, Roe's son called him to tell him how busy the restaurant was that night, when he hung the telephone up, he told Louis what his son had called to tell him, when he told Louis the name of the restaurant, Louis said that's where he had dinner at every Friday night, Roe said I own it, and he gave Louis a special V.I.P. card, that when used, he would get special parking privileges and would never have to make reservations or wait on a table when dining there.

14

"PROPER PERSPECTIVES"

1ST Corinthians 14:40

"Let all things be done decently and in order"

2nd Corinthians 4:17-18

"For our light affliction, which is but for a moment, worketh for us a far more exceeding and eternal weight of glory. While we look not at the things which are seen, but at the things which are not seen: for the things which are seen are temporal; but the things which are not seen are eternal."

1st Timothy 6:6

"But godliness with contentment is great gain."

Louis had always felt, that although to others he may have appeared to have it all together, God knew, and he and God also knew of the inner demons that had for so long plagued him in his life, that were it not for God, they would have destroyed him a long time ago. We as a people must realize, that God is God, and it is because of his grace, that if we are anything at all, God alone deserves all glory and praise.

Even now, Louis was not totally content being back at his home church, although it had been where he was born and raised at, he realized that sometimes a change can do an individual a world of good. Louis was determined to stay put until he felt the divine leading of God's omnipotent hand. He was not alone in his discontentment there, many of those that had been there at the church for a great many years, had already left, as can usually be expected with the changing of the guard, when one leaders dies out, or leaves the church for whatever reason, and a new leader comes in and takes over, many of the things that people had grown accustomed to, will generally change, the traditions and doctrines of a church can also differ greatly from one individual pastor to another, although it's true that there is only one God, our individual perception of him will differ drastically, leaving some thinking that they are in more of a right standing with God, than others that are in the same church.

Louis had been a deacon at the church for the past ten years, Elder Logan now refused to renew his license, even this did not bother Louis, the truth is, that he probably knew the business of the church as well as anyone else in the congregation. Through it all he was just as faithful with his time and his finances, as he had always been. He would often talk to his parents and ask them couldn't they see that things weren't right in the church, like many others, they always tried to see the best in everyone, and many things they said, born again Christians just would not do.

Louis had always wished that he could do more for his parents, one of the greatest things that he had done for them, as we had discussed earlier about Al Timm's not holding on to a job early on in his life. Well Louis went and found Al a job, at the age of Fifty seven years old, not only Al, they even hired Edith, well now after working ten years, bless God, they were both fully vested, and were now both able to retire with a full pension.

The Timm's children decided that for their parents fiftieth anniversary, which was now fast approaching, they would throw them the event of the century, and they did just that. Louis rented a stretch limousine for the two of them, the children rented a hall, they had it all very elegantly catered, they even decorated the church and planned a big ceremony for them to renew their vows, which they did, the children had invited relatives from all over, everything was simply beautiful, this was the wedding that Edith said, she had always wanted but had never had.

Now that they were retired, Al and Edith could really enjoy a life of leisure, they were now able to travel extensively, but what Edith said she enjoyed more than anything, was the fact that they could now be at the church every time the doors were opened, as well as being able to go to the many out of town meetings that the church held throughout the year, this she would often say, was her little taste of heaven right here on earth.

2 Chronicles 16:9

"For the eyes of the Lord run to and fro throughout the whole earth, to shew himself strong in the behalf of them whose heart is perfect toward him. Herein thou hast done foolishly: therefore from henceforth thou shalt have wars."

The many conventions that the church held throughout the year, were another point of contention. There are many sincere individuals that desire to serve and to please God, but this does not negate the fact, that there are also many others that use the church as a cloak to do and to hide their wickedness, not realizing that God has an all seeing eye. Many of the new members, that were very sincere, as most are when they first join the church, would wonder to themselves, why is it that late at night at these conventions, they often see people either going into, or coming out of someone else's hotel room, that they knew was not the individuals spouse, many of the individuals going to these various meetings, would have been terribly upset if their spouses had gone with them, just for this reason.

Others now began to see problems creeping into the church, as well as with Pastor Logan's leadership, the same problems that Louis had earlier tried to tell his parents about. Things were beginning to get out of kilter, questions began to arise, that upset the dictatorial attitude that plagues some churches, and once again, more people began to leave the church.

One evening while Louis was visiting the sick in one of the local hospitals, as he was leaving, he walked past the waiting room on his way to the elevator, and out of the waiting room he heard someone call, hey Brother Timm's, as he turned he could see that it was Brother Robinson, one of the members from the church that he had left, when he and Carol had divorced, whom he had not seen in about six years. He told Louis that there had been so many problems since he had left their church, and that they had finally, after all these years gotten rid of Pastor Carl Evans, he also told Louis, that Carol was now gone also.

The predicament that Pastor Evans had gotten himself into, is common to that of many a pastor, who in an effort to counsel or to console an individual, we tend to explore our limitations, seeing just how far an individual will allow us to go, many a Pastor has gotten himself into more trouble than he can get himself out of just because of this, when we lack the proper integrity that is needed for this kind of an office, we can open the door to what could potentially be spiritual, emotional, mental and even possibly physical problems, this, on the part of both parties involved.

Now Pastor Evans had been counseling a woman at the church named Gwen, Louis knew her well, now remember, not only had Pastor Evans been married for approximately a quarter century, he and his wife also had a son, Gwen was no better, she had a husband and three daughters, and it seemed that for a good long while, she needed counseling more than anybody else at the church. Well however things went down, and nobody really knows but the two of them, one thing led to another and Gwen left her husband, next thing you know, after twenty five years of marriage, Pastor Evans just could not tolerate living in the house with his wife any longer, therefore he moved out, conveniently into the same apartment complex that Gwen had moved into, didn't I tell you

"CHURCH-FOLK SOME MESSED-UP-FOLK"

Louis now decided that he would began to put things in order, that he might once again be able to return to this church, now that he had heard that Pastor Evans was gone. He told his parents and his wife of his intentions, he also told his wife that he was doing what was best for him spiritually, he also told Tina that he would put no demands on her to go with him, he was simply doing what was best for him at this time, still praying that he would be led by the divine hand and spirit of the living God.

It was about two and a half months before Louis finally had himself situated to return to that church, but he did, and Tina went with him, many of the older people that were still there, were very happy to see him return, a few were not, one woman even told Louis that she could not believe that he had the nerve to show his face there again, you see the story that had been told to them, was that Louis had put his wife and children out, and had married his mistress, with whom he had been carrying on an affair for many years, Louis told her that this was not the truth, he also said that he did not feel that he had to prove himself to anyone. I can tell you beyond a shadow of a doubt, there simply was no truth at all in any of this.

Louis actually arrived back at that church, the Sunday before the new Pastor was to arrive himself, this was all a part of God's plan for Louis at this time in his life. The following week when the new Pastor arrived, he and Louis hit it off immediately, his name was Pastor Jerome Bradshaw, he had a wife and two children. This was his first Pastorate, and he relied very heavily on Louis to help him run things, not exactly sure of what else Louis had going on in his life, Pastor Bradshaw urged Louis to take the necessary courses and become licensed in that organization, which he did.

Louis also he received his Master of Business Administration degree, majoring in Accounting that same year, he had decided that since he loved to read and to study, that he may as well make the most of them both. He received a couple of job offers elsewhere, but he told them that he was not interested, he wasn't doing this for the money, he was looking at a much bigger picture, he was doing this for God.

Exodus 33:13

"Now therefore, I pray thee, if I have found grace in thy sight, shew me now thy way, that I may know thee, that I may find grace in thy sight: and consider that this nation is thy people."

Matthew 22:14

"For many are called, but few are chosen"

That same year that Louis changed churches, if you'll remember, Louis's job had split into two companies, well now, the smaller one that Louis had been sent to work at, had been losing a great deal of money, so in a move that took everyone totally by surprise, it was sold off to a large conglomerate. All the employees were now told that if they could not find a position back at the larger company, their employment would now transfer to the conglomerate that had purchased them, this sent everyone scrambling for one position that had come up, eighty eight applicants applied for this one position, many were called in for interviews, but Louis was that chosen one.

Psalm 8:4

"What is man, that thou art mindful of him? and the son of man, that thou visitest him?"

This shows that there is a reality in walking according to God's word, Louis was not really expecting the job, not that he didn't want it, he was not anxious for it, knowing all along that God had a place for him somewhere, and many have lost out not realizing this.

Louis received a telephone call from someone asking him if he had heard that after nearly twenty years on her job, Carol had gotten fired for stealing, which he had not, the individual calling was supposing that this would please Louis, it did not, he told them that he would pray for her, and true to his word, he did just that.

The following year, Louis's parents also told him that problems had also escalated at their church, now to a point of no return, the members had signed and circulated a petition to oust their Pastor, Pastor Logan, it took three months but they were finally able to get rid of him, leaving Minister Al Timm's as the new Pastor, again politics crept in, leaving Louis sorely displeased, this we may discuss a little later.

Edith and Al Timm's were no longer that young, and both, now gradually began to experience their health fail. Edith had been a diabetic for many years, and now she had just been diagnosed with an incurable form of cancer, never wanting to worry her family, she had been quiet about certain problems she had been experiencing for months, now the entire family was informed, Edith had always been a fighter, she now had a long hard journey ahead of her, as well as the rest of the family.

Acts 20:35

"I have shewed you all things, how that so labouring ye ought to support the weak, and to remember the words of the Lord Jesus, how he said, it is more blessed to give than to receive."

That Christmas, as he had done for so many of the past years, Louis gave thousands of dollars away to the needy, mostly in the church. This is something that I had always done, and had always told Louis that most people don't understand that God's laws of physics in this area are very different than man's, the more you give, the more God will bless you, and the tighter that you try to hold on to that which you have, you'll find that it almost takes evasive maneuvers.

Having completed the necessary class work and the examinations that were required, Louis was not only licensed by the church that he was now attending, but he was also appointed by the overseer as the assisting minister, in addition to this he was also sanctioned by the state to perform weddings and funerals, for this, he was ever so grateful to Pastor Bradshaw for suggesting that he do this in the first place.

Now back at his parents church, they were not nearly as structured, a ministers license there was much easier to obtain, but it was never something that God had impressed upon Louis's heart to seek there, or to even want, when I came along all you had to do was to say that you were a preacher, and you were given a license, now they do at least make you take a test first. This was one of the things that had also had stuck out in Louis's mind, I would often tell him about these little jackleg or bootleg preachers, which is how I referred to them, that were just out looking for a title. As Louis's life progressed, I often saw things affirming that I was influencing his life in some manner.

That following year, as Al and Edith Timm's anniversary rolled around once again, which was on February 28th, Louis and the other children again began to prepare for a large celebration for their parents, the date that they had chosen for all of the festivities was Saturday March 2nd, 2002, however, as fate would have it, or God, two of the sisters had already planned a trip for that weekend and would be out of town, therefore the following Saturday, being March 9TH was chosen.

Let me regress for a moment, there is no such thing as fate, everything is as it should be in the plan of the divine God, if it wasn't, it wouldn't be. In this, I am specifically speaking of the original date that the Timm's children wanted to commemorate their parents anniversary. That particular Saturday, March 2nd, Louis got a call from his father, it seems that Edith had blacked out, and Al had called "911", they were now there working on her, trying to get her to respond, Louis immediately left his home, and headed for his parents home.

Before he ever arrived at there home, he saw his father following the ambulance, Louis parked his vehicle, jumped into the car with his father, and off they continued to the hospital. Once they arrived, they took Edith on in and continued working on her, while Louis and Al waited anxiously in the waiting room. After about half an hour, a nurse came out and told them that the two of them could go on back to see her. As the two of them walked through the long corridor, Louis mind was racing, as any individual knows, you only get one mother, and until you actually lose her, you simply cannot imagine life without her, Louis prayed that God would intervene and that Edith would be alright, because aside from God alone, there was no hope.

As Louis and Al walked in, they could see that Edith did not look well, Louis grabbed her hand and asked her what happened, I don't know she told him, Al told her that she had really frightened him. As Louis stood there talking to her, she said that she felt so strange, her feet were bothering her, she needed to get out of the bed and go for a walk, Louis told her that she couldn't because she had all of these tubes tied up to her, and as Louis stood there holding her hand, he could feel her going limp, he looked into her face as her eyes rolled back into her head and one monitor began to beep, while the other one flat lined, it was 6:05 P.M., and two doctors and three nurses ran into the room and asked everyone to leave the room, and they pulled the curtains closed.

James 5:14

"Is any sick among you? Let him call for the elders of the church; and let them pray over him, anointing him with oil in the name of the Lord: And the prayer of faith shall save the sick, and the Lord shall raise him up; and if he have committed sins, they shall be forgiven him."

Standing there outside of those curtains, Louis prayed as he had never prayed before, begging God to please not take their mother away from them. Now exactly when is it a good time to lose one's mother. There is nothing that can compare to a true mothers love, it leaves a void that can almost be compared to the ripping away of your very soul, the finality of it all can be most overwhelming. A true mother, when the whole world has given up on you, she still clings to her hope that you'll one day make something out of your life, however vile an individual may be, a true mothers love, keeps her praying to God for grace, mercy and salvation, a true mother has gone without, sacrificing that which was a genuine need, to provide for the frivolous wants of a pouting child.

After about ten minutes they all came out, one of the doctors told Al and Louis that they couldn't explain what had happened, but that she had died, but miraculously she had come back around, and that the two of them could now go in and see her, once again the two of them went in to see Edith, Louis could also see that Al was visibly shaken by all of this, and his prayers were for him as well, neither Al, nor Edith would function very well without the other, they were soul mates.

Upon seeing Edith this time, she seemed to be doing a little better, she was not fully aware of all that had gone on though, but she was talking fine now and everything appeared to be okay. The doctors could not explain any of this, and after a battery of tests, that all revealed nothing out of the ordinary, they were even more puzzled. Even though up to this point they could find nothing wrong, they said that they would still like to keep her overnight just for observation.

Edith later told Louis that the whole evening that this entire event took place was a blank to her, she said that she remembered being at home eating that previous afternoon, and the next that thing she remembered was waking up in the hospital the next morning.

After this, Edith was discharged from the hospital. The children talked to her and told her that perhaps they should cancel the big anniversary dinner that had been planned for that Saturday, Edith said no, she insisted that it go on like none of this had happened. Edith had always loved it when the children did this sort of thing, not so much for herself, but for the fellowship that it provided the entire family, they were not a perfect family, but she knew how she had raised them, she also knew that when she was no longer around, this close knit family that she had always loved and prayed for, would not have the same sense of commitment to God, or to one another.

One thing that Edith had never wanted, was for anyone to treat her like an invalid, even when she honestly did need the help, she told them that she would rather try and do certain things on her own, she had always been an independent woman, able to fend for herself and her family, and to always get by on very little, all the while being most grateful for whatever she and her family had. It had taken Al a very long time, before he finally realized and truly appreciated that what he had was a rare and precious jewel, but now, he couldn't imagine his life without her.

Psalm 84:11

"For the Lord God is a sun and shield: the Lord will give grace and glory: no good thing will he withhold from them that walk uprightly."

That Saturday, March 9th, the Timm's children threw their parents one of the most beautiful anniversary dinners that anyone could have ever imagined, there were many friends of the family there, relatives and a host of church members also lined the place, Edith and Al were most pleased. The children had even rented them a suite, with a Jacuzzi in it, Edith loved this she said most of all, once she had gotten into it, she even asked the children, what would it cost to have one of these installed at our home?

That same summer, the church that Louis now belonged to, had a pastor resign, and word had gotten back to Louis, that since he had already gone through and passed their strict licensing process, which also included an in depth background and fingerprint check, the governing board there, felt that he might be the perfect candidate to now pastor this small church. These background checks were something that our church had not been nearly as thorough in doing.

Psalm 27:14

"Wait on the Lord: be of good courage, and he shall strengthen thine heart: wait, I say, on the Lord."

This, some might think, was the perfect opportunity for someone that now possessed the credentials that Louis had, not Louis, he told them that he wasn't interested, he knew that there were things and areas of his life, that God was still at work in, and one thing that he had always said to himself, was that he didn't want to be one that was guilty of running out ahead of God, simply because a need is there, this doesn't necessarily mean that God wants you to fill it, Louis was determined to wait on God's blessed assurance that he was in the place that God wanted him to be.

Philippians 3:7-8

"But what things were gain to me, those I counted loss for Christ. Yea doubtless, and I count all things but loss for the excellency of the knowledge of Christ Jesus my Lord: for whom I have suffered the loss of all things, and do count them but dung, that I may win Christ."

The latter part of that same year, being just about done with his quest for knowledge, Louis received his Doctor of Philosophy degree, majoring in Biblical Studies, he had started out with a different major, but he now felt that the way the spirit of God was dealing with him, he asked could he change it before he had gone to far through the year, and he was allowed to do so by the school. Would you believe that after this he still signed up for more classes. Louis had seen too many individuals, that wanted to be in the ministry just for the money, Louis had always dreamed of a church, where offerings were not even taken up, a box would simply be placed at the door, where according to God's leading and blessing, individuals would utilize it, and as they were leaving the church after each service, would simply follow God's leading, according to how he had blessed them.

Many would commend Louis on his job, asking him did he have a college degree, he would simply reply, his schooling is totally unrelated to his job. Christ was, and is his true treasure, anything that this world has to offer him, pales in comparison to this. His glory is in this, that he knows the Lord Jesus Christ, in the free pardon of his sins. Of this alone, he is most grateful.

15

"IT IS WELL, WITH MY SOUL"

Galatians 5:7

"Ye did run well; who did hinder you that ye should not obey the truth"

Ecclesiastes 12:13-14

"Let us hear the conclusion of the whole matter: fear God, and keep his commandments: for this is the whole duty of man. For God shall bring every work into judgment, with every secret thing, whether it be good, or whether it be evil."

Louis, after leading what he had felt up until this time was a very tumultuous life, now felt that things were going halfway right. He could finally, just now somewhat understand and appreciate all of the things God had taken him through, how can you truly tell others where God has brought you from, telling them that you are a living witness to the miraculous saving power of God, if you don't know this experientially. How can you tell someone, about the grace of a God that can deliver them, if you've never been in dire straits yourself and had to call on him in your own time of need.

I know that we haven't said much about them, but Maeline, Junior and Byron are all grown now. The three of them graduated from high school, and went on to further studies, Maeline and Byron also received college degrees, and God blessed them with very good jobs. Junior went into a trade program after he graduated and got a job working for the government.

James 5:16

"Confess your faults one to another, and pray one for another, that ye may be healed. The effectual fervent prayer of a righteous man availeth much."

Al and Edith Timm's even now, are still both doing reasonably well. June of that following year however, Edith was put under hospice care and was told that she had approximately six months to live, by the nurse that had been put in charge of her case, Louis sat there and listened to the nurse talk to Edith, she explained that she had been a hospice nurse for the past fifteen years, she knew that this was not an easy thing to do, but looking at Edith's records, she told the family that her body was now beginning to shut down, and that whereas the normal blood count was over one hundred and forty, Edith's had progressively gone down, and was somewhere around thirty seven right now. Edith and Al both, sitting there now listening, crying like babies by this time.

Louis told his siblings that he thought that they should all pray for their mother and go on a fast the entire month of July. Would you believe that not one of them was willing to do this with him. Louis did it alone, he first mentally prepared himself, he then told his wife so that she would be aware of the fact that he would not be eating any food, then when July 1st came around, he went over and anointed Edith with oil and prayed for her, he then left and began his fast.

Some of his family members asked why would you start a fast in July, with the holiday right around the corner, well Louis asked, is it any good time to start a fast. That July 4th, Louis, Tina and Eljay went to their families picnic where food was in an over abundance as usual, Louis sat there and watched, as they all gorged themselves with food, some even trying to entice Louis with the fine delicacies that were normally there, this if anything gave Louis all the more power to resist.

This he felt, and rightly so, was a fast that God had chosen, not just for Edith, but just as much for Louis. God wanted him to know that he was and is still in the healing business. Louis had tried to fast for long periods before, with little, or no success when doing it for himself, but for mother, it was now a different story. Louis lost twenty five pounds, and the fasting never bothered him at all. Each week Louis would go over and anoint Edith with oil and pray for her, believing God for a miracle.

Now just as when certain illnesses began to attack our bodies, we have no idea what's going on inside of us, until it manifests itself in one way or another, some sicknesses attack the body very rapidly, while with others the process is a very gradual one. When Robert Timm's had died, by the time the family found out that he even had cancer, it had ravaged his body so badly, that the majority of doctors that saw him said that they felt there was very little hope, if any at all. We must remember that there is a price to pay for sin.

Louis knew that God was a miracle worker, he also knew that God did not always intervene, God's answers can be yes, no or wait, and which one was not always an easy thing to discern. Whatever God's answers might be to us, we must always know, that in every situation, he is able, there are only two things that God cannot do, he cannot lie, and he cannot fail.

Edith now normally had doctor appointments about three days a week. That August, Louis asked her how things were going and she said that they were about the same, she told Louis that God had given her what he had promised her, threescore and ten years, and that she could not expect to live forever. That September, once again Louis asked and she told him that things had not changed that much, Edith even told Louis that she almost wanted to die, just to retire the pin cushions that she now felt her arms had become.

Daniel 10:12-13

"Then said he unto me, Fear not, Daniel: for from the first day that thou didst set thine heart to understand, and to chasten thyself before thy God, thy words were heard, and I am come for thy words. But the prince of the kingdom of Persia withstood me one and twenty days: but, lo, Michael, one of the chief princes, came to help me; and I remained there with the kings of Persia."

Louis said that he was holding out until God blessed in this situation, just as God had sent an answer to Daniel, Louis said that delay is not denial, and he kept right on praying, two of the main tricks that the devil uses is deceit and procrastination, trying to make us think that not only does the Lord not hear us, but neither is he concerned with us, this, to try and make us lose heart, and faint, just when we might have broken through, and been given the victory.

This brought to Louis's mind the story of a mountain climber that he had once heard, this climber was going up the mountain, doing all of the proper things that a mountain climber knows to do, when night began to fall, and I don't know about you, but most mountains do not have lights on them for night climbing, and the nights can be very dark, well as he continued to climb, it seemed that he just was not coming across anywhere that he might find a level ledge, to rest until the next morning, also the cold was very brutal at night.

This mountain climber lost his footing, and as he began to fall, he also shifted about eight feet to the side of this mountain, try as he might, he could find anything at all to grab on to, this climber prayed heaven down that night, and beseeching God for deliverance, he heard a still small voice saying let go of the rope, afraid, he held on to it all that much tighter. The next morning, a group of five other climbers found him, frozen to death, still tightly holding on to the rope, his feet were hanging six inches above a sturdy landing. If he had only let go of the rope.

That October, things had began to look much better, the doctors got the test results in, and they called Edith to tell her that they needed her to come back in for some additional tests, thinking that something was wrong with their equipment. What the doctors did not tell Edith, was that the tests showed her blood count had now jumped from in the thirties, to in the seventies, this was most unusual. Isn't it just like God to reverse the negative situations in our lives, even today.

That October, upon Edith's return to the hospital, the tests results came out exactly the same way, there was nothing wrong with their equipment, the doctors now contacted hospice, and Edith was removed from hospice care. That November, Edith's blood count was one hundred and nine, and they now said that the cancer cells were even disappearing. That December, her blood count was one hundred and thirty two, now come on people, who wouldn't serve a God like this.

By January that following year, Edith's blood count was one hundred and forty five, the doctors ran three separate tests that week, they were stunned, they said that they could no longer find any cancer cells anywhere. Although she said that for the most part, she still did not feel the greatest, the doctors told her that these were just normal old age problems, that had nothing to do with the cancer that had once plagued her body.

God has given Louis a special gift, however he lets self get in the way, and refuses to exercise it. He's too busy looking at church-folk, letting them cloud his thinking, he prays about this continually, that the Lord will help him to look past an individuals faults, and see their needs. He has been reprimanded by many, for sitting on this gift. One woman confided in Louis that she had chronic back pains and had been on disability for years, she had asked Louis to pray for her once, and she immediately said she felt her healing, she also later confided in Louis, that feeling fine, and being convicted, she had her disability stopped, and went back to work.

The weekly ritual of having dinner at the Timm's home every Saturday, continues until this day. A couple of the weeks right before Christmas, when Louis was there, he happened to notice that there were automobiles magazines laying around, that his father had been looking at. One Saturday upon leaving their home, God began speaking to Louis, letting him know that you only get one set of parents, when they are dead and gone, it's too late to say what you wish you would have done, that which we have the means and power to do, that we should do.

When Louis arrived home that very night, he called back over to his parents home, he told his father that he had been seeing these automobile magazines laying around and was wondering if he was planning on buying a new car, Al told him that he was just looking, he said that he would love to be able to say that he had one nice car before he died, but he knew that he could not afford one. That night Louis did not rest well at all, just thinking about what his father had said to him. That Sunday after church, although he knew the car dealers were all closed, he went out looking for his father a car anyway, and he found one, he prayed about it, and then he went back home.

The following Monday morning Louis went on to work, he went back to the same lot where he had seen this car, he test drove it, he explained to the salesperson why he wanted to purchase the car and he made them an offer, the salesperson told Louis that he would have to talk to the owner, and he was called in, again Louis explained to the owner that he wanted to buy this car for his ailing father and told him what he was willing to pay, Louis had always seen God's handiwork in his life, and with this it would be no different.

It was as if God had truly gone in and prepared the way, without exchanging any words at all, he asked Louis how had he planned to pay for it and who's name would he like the automobile to be titled in, Louis told him that he would pay for the car in full, right there on the spot, and that it should be titled it in the name of Al Timm's, Louis explained to him that he was on his lunch break, and that if he could have the vehicle prepped and all the paperwork done by 4:00 P.M., that he would bring his father back to pick it up then, the owner assured him that it would be ready.

Louis went back to work and called his father, he asked him what he had planned for the remainder of the day, once Al told him that he had no plans, Louis told him that he needed him to pick him up from work. Once Al arrived at Louis's place of employment, Louis directed him where the two of them needed to go.

Upon pulling into the dealership, Louis could see the car sitting out front, as they exited the vehicle, Al still unaware of what was going on as Louis pointed to the vehicle and said isn't that a nice one, Al looked at it and said that it was beautiful, just as the salesperson was coming out to greet them, Louis then said, well it's yours, Al thought that he was joking, he was given the keys to take the car for a test drive, which he did. When he returned, the salesperson told him that the car had already been paid for in full, and that all he needed to do was to come in and sign some paperwork, and that then he could take his new Lincoln Towne Car home.

Louis could see the tears of joy in his fathers eyes as he filled in all of the necessary information, he could her the sounds of unbelief in his voice as he told Louis how much he appreciated this. Just the look on his fathers face was enough for Louis, to see a grown man weeping like a baby, thinking that someone loves me this much.

Romans 5:8

"But God commendeth his love toward us, in that, while we were yet sinners, Christ died for us."

How much more has God done for each and every one of us, not because of, but in spite of, it was his grace that kept us from getting what we truly deserved. When our sins, though as black as could be, kept us separated from a holy and righteous God, he left his throne in glory and came down to pay a debt that he didn't owe, to satisfy our debt that we owed, and couldn't pay, it was Jesus who paid it all, he gave his all for each and every one of us. Our very life is a gift from God, how we live it, is our gift back to him.

A few months after this, Louis had finally learned one of the hardest lessons of his life, after co-signing for someone in the church, he received paperwork from the courts, that this saved, sanctified, Holy Ghost filled, fire baptized saint, had not been properly handling their business affairs, and now Louis was being sued by a large company for forty five thousand dollars, he immediately called his attorney and forwarded all of the information on to him, there was nothing that could be done, Louis had to pay his hard earned money. Need I tell you one last time

"CHURCH-FOLK SOME MESSED-UP-FOLK"

This was the final straw, Louis told his mother, that if someone came to him in need, if he couldn't give them a little something to help out, they would just be out of luck, after being stuck like this, he assured his parents that he wouldn't co-sign for anyone else a hotdog, this he said was a hard pill to swallow. People act like they don't understand why an individual may grow cold and callous, too many of us are reading the new reversed version of scripture, we are loving things and using people, this is not the way God intended for it to be.

There's nothing at all wrong with helping, or even wanting to help someone out, however we must gauge our own selves, there are certain individuals, even in our own families, that given the very thought that we may have a little money, will do everything within their power, to try and get it away from us. Louis was very wise in this matter, and the one thing that he was determined to do, was to not touch the money that I had left for him, and until this very day, he still has it in a special account.

It is not a good feeling to know that you have been wronged by an individual, especially when they can continue to walk all over and around you, as if nothing is wrong, fear not, the redeemed of the Lord have a great avenger, God is not dead, neither does he sleep.

Throughout his lifetime, although things were not always easy, however, Louis was determined that he would not sacrifice that which was eternal, for that which is only temporary. We must look beyond our self gratifying worldly indulgences, that left to our own devices, we would soon allow them to destroy us. We must live our lives with eternity in view, the bible is not a book telling us how to live in heaven, it tells us how we **must** live right here in this present age, that is if we really want heaven as our eternal home.

Now if we really don't care about reigning with the Lord Jesus throughout all of eternity, if we are really not appreciative for what the Lord Jesus Christ has done for us, then neither the bible nor this book is for you, just continue to live as though you are going to live always. Why go to hell in a wheel barrel, when you can go in a Cadillac, don't cheat and short change yourself in this life and in the life to come, just know this, we shall all stand before the judgment seat of Christ, where every man will be paid according to his works.

Tina's cousin Donald, and his wife Dinah, were pastors of one of the local churches here, a beautiful couple that seemed to have it all. One of the couples in the church had began to have marital problems, Donald, being the Pastor, had began counseling them, and the problems, if anything, seemed to have gotten worse. The husband called Dinah one day to tell her that his wife was pregnant, not that strange, except he told Dinah that after their fourth child he had gotten a vasectomy. Yes you know what happened, during one of these counseling session, this young, married Pastor, had impregnated another man's wife. These

"CHURCH-FOLK SOME MESSED-UP FOLK"

Dinah was livid, she divorced Donald, moved away, and purposed to just get on with the rest of her life. Donald would go over to see their children, always pleading and begging for forgiveness. After about a year of this, he wore Dinah's resistance down, and she forgave him, and the two of them were remarried. Now isn't God good, aren't we glad that he is the God of second chances, and third chances, and fourth chances.

Well God may be good, but we've certainly got some problems with our messed up lives, less than one year after remarrying Donald, would you believe that Dinah found out this same woman was pregnant by Donald again. This time Dinah divorced him and moved out of the country. Yes,

"CHURCH-FOLK SOME MESSED-UP-FOLK"

We live in an age where there is too little accountability, every man has gone after his own ways, even preachers, who can stand in the pulpit of many a church, on any given Sunday morning, some even preaching the unadulterated word of God, are guilty of some of the vilest of sins, simply because they have no one to call them into question about it, what about God, he sits high and he looks low, we will all, one day give an account of all that we have done, to the omniscient God.

Bishop Bright, if you will recall, was the Chief Disciple that had taken over as head of our organization upon the founders death, he had a good long run, staying in power for approximately twenty five tumultuous years, his entire family has prospered well beyond what most Christians could even imagine. They all now lived in mansions, in one of the most exclusive suburbs in their city, and they drove some of the most expensive luxury cars that money can buy.

Now looking back at church doctrine and by-laws, as we earlier discussed, Bishop Bright should never have held on to this position for this long of a time. Age has now taken its toll on him, he was only five years younger than myself. One of the by-laws mandated by the founder, was that a woman could never be a Bishop, neither could she be head of this great organization, this office had to be held by an ordained Bishop,

Bishop Bright was well into his eighties, when he made his daughter his assistant pastor. They, being him and his immediate family, were now trying to get the board of Bishops to change the church by-laws, to allow women, to now hold the office of a Bishop, if they could accomplish this, they would then be able to move her in as Bishop Bright's successor, something that the founding Bishop never intended, but yes politics have crept into our churches.

When the Bright family could not accomplish this evil that they had purposed in their hearts, they then began siphoning money out of the churches accounts, and by the time anyone was willing to question things, Bishop Bright had now become somewhat incapacitated, and the church accounts were now short over five million dollars. This is the kind of thing that even makes people outside of the church feel, and rightfully so, that

"CHURCH-FOLK SOME MESSED-UP-FOLK"

All of this, combined with self righteous individuals, still unwilling to be accountable to anyone, caused one of the largest church splits of this century, and lawsuits, that after three years, are still going on.

Louis has seen more than his share of corruption, in and out of the church, he thinks that especially those in leadership positions, have a moral obligation to God and to man, to walk worthy of the position that has been entrusted unto them, as of the writing of this book, Louis said that every Pastor or Christian counselor, should put up money out of their own pockets, to be forfeited in the event that some sexual indiscretion is uncovered in their lives, and he challenges them with this, as of the writing of this book, there is a standing offer to any woman that can bring any past, or present, bonafide charge of sexual misconduct of any kind, against Dr. Louis Timm's.

To those smart individuals that may say, this offer is to women only, how astute of you, in this day and age this point is well taken, to any man that can bring any past or present, bonafide charge of any sexual misconduct, this offer is doubled, to twenty thousand dollars. All I'm trying to say is, there simply needs to be more accountability.

I am fully persuaded that Louis can now take care of himself, with the help of the Lord. All that I desire and have always desired, was that he would be the great man of God that I know that he was destined to be, that the Lord would use him and do great and marvelous things through him. That he will go on to know him in a more intimate way, the more that his life progresses. I know that one day my son in the gospel and I, will be reunited, where we will reign with the King of Kings, and Lords of Lords, throughout all eternity.

My time is up, God has given me my hearts desire, that I might be a positive influence in this young mans life, that my words would continue to lead and guide him, as they have these past fifteen years, that I would always have a place in his heart, as the "Beloved Bishop", my work is done, I now feel that my spirit can be at rest, I now go on to that blessed place.

Genesis 31:49

"And Mizpah; for he said, The Lord watch between me and thee, when we are absent one from another."

"MIZPAH"

CONCLUSION

Ecclesiastes 1:2

"Vanity of vanities, saith the Preacher, vanity of vanities, all is vanity."

Ecclesiastes 12:13-14

"Let us hear the conclusion of the whole matter: Fear God, and keep his commandments: for this is the whole duty of man. For God shall bring every work into judgment, with every secret thing, whether it be good, or whether it be evil."

Galatians 5:7

"Ye did run well; who did hinder you that you should not obey the truth?"

There is a reality in worshiping the one true God. Gods heartfelt desire is for those that worship him, to worship him in spirit and truth, with their whole heart, mind, body and soul, to cast off everything that's not like him. God is still searching for men and women who are willing to exemplify a Christ like character, in their everyday lives, willing to go against the grain of the societal dictates that govern the rest of the world, and what it calls success, to a selfless life of love and obedience to God and commandments.

Proverbs 4:7

"Wisdom is the principal thing; therefore get wisdom: and with all thy getting get understanding."

Aside from life in Jesus Christ, there is no life at all, just emptiness.

Titus 3:3-4

"For we ourselves also were sometimes foolish, disobedient, deceived, serving divers lusts and pleasures, living in malice and envy, hateful, and hating one another."

1ˢᵗ Corinthians 6:9-11

"Know ye not that the unrighteous shall not inherit the kingdom of God? Be not deceived: neither fornicators, nor idolaters, nor adulterers, nor effeminate, nor abusers of themselves with mankind, Nor thieves, nor covetous, nor drunkards, nor revilers, nor extortioners, shall inherit the kingdom of God. And such were some of you: but ye are washed, but ye are sanctified, but ye are justified in the name of the Lord Jesus, and by the Spirit of our God."

No one has any room at all to talk about anyone else, because there but for the grace of God they would still be. Nobody has been saved all of their life, contrary to what they might try to make you think, all were born in sin, and all have sinned. The problem is that too many of us have forgotten where we came from, some of our halo's are on a little too tight, and it has began to effect our thinking. God still saves. Won't you accept his gift today.

If you are not in right standing with God right now, invite him in, confess with your mouth that Jesus is your Lord, acknowledge that you are a sinner in need of a Saviour, ask him to forgive you for your sins, past, present and future, believe that the Lord Jesus died for you and your sins, and that you are now covered by his shed blood on Calvary, ask him to be the Lord of your life and take up residency in your heart, to rest rule and abide with you both now and forevermore, to lead you, with his divine hand as only he can.

0-595-33230-7